PIECES

PLAYS: 1

ACKNOWLEDGEMENTS

The author would like to thank all those who have helped to support the writing and performance of these plays. This includes people who've given feedback on plays in progress, workshop leaders, authors of books on playwrighting, members of each production, audience members, Holly at Alma Tavern Theatre, James Peries, Matt Grinter, Knight Writers, and Maddie Marzola and Euphoria Kew for valuable feedback on the design of this book.

This collection first published in 2021 by Magnetical.

e-mail: hello@magnetical.com

www.magnetical.com

A catalogue record for this book is available from the British Library.

Printed and bound in the United Kingdom by Ingram Spark.

Designed by James Pople

Proofread by Clare Diston

ISBN: 9781916064638

Printed and bound by Ingram Spark.

PIECES
PLAYS: 1

**MERLIN
GOLDMAN**

MAGNETICAL

A CHRONOLOGY

2016–17 *Killing Rainbows* was first performed in 2016 in the Alma Tavern Theatre, directed by Daniel Smith. Its next performance was above Bordeaux Quay restaurant, directed by June Trask. It's third in 2017 was above the White Bear pub in Cotham and directed by Kris Hallett. All performances were in Bristol, UK.

2016 *Our Kid* was longlisted for the Pint-sized Plays competition.

2017 *Tick-Tock* and *TANK* were directed by Daniel Smith and performed as part of an evening of plays (Pantomime Shorts) at the Alma Tavern Theatre.

2019 *A Game of Two Halves* was written during a playwriting course run by Matt Grinter at Theatre Royal Bath. This culminated with all the pieces being performed for one night in the main auditorium. It was directed by Chloe Masterton.

2019 *Hit Points* was shortlisted in Bristol Old Vic's Open Session.

2020 *Chainsaw* was directed by Michelle Parker and shown at The King's Arms Theatre in Salford, UK.

2016–20 The premise of *Loud Mouth* was longlisted for The Old Vic 12 in 2016 and completed in 2020.

CONTENTS

INTRODUCTION

The first play I wrote was called *Firewall* and was
performed in 2007 at Club Lambi for two nights as part
of the Indyish Assembly 2.0 International Collaborative
Art Relay at the Montreal Fringe Festival. Writers around
the world created scripts based on a never-before-seen
T J Dawe piece. Scripts were passed in a relay with close to
100 illustrators, animators, actors and musicians. Artists
changed the pieces as much as they wanted while working
under a time limit. Unfortunately, the original and final
script were both lost.

Killing Rainbows was inspired by a conversation I had
with Chris Chalkey as part of a creative workshop held in
his building in Stokes Croft. He told us how he'd taken
pride in the area, sweeping the pavement outside. He
began painting anti-consumerist slogans on billboards
and walls, which led him into conflict with Bristol City
Council. They would send staff to cover the artwork with
grey squares. His life story inspired the play. To have the
play performed three times allowed me to tweak it each

time, strengthening the story engine as I learnt more about storytelling.

Our Kid was written in response to the killing of journalists by jihadi terrorists. I was never brave enough to watch the videos, but the horror of the events sickened me enough to channel it into a play. Several of the most notorious kidnappers were British and it struck me as perverse that there might be two British men, locked together in a room on foreign shores, with their lives at stake. And what if they found out that they were from the same town and had the same interests? 'What if?' The spark that starts a writer's creative journey.

TANK and *Tick-Tock* were written for a self-produced night of shorts. Dreamt up over a pizza with Euphoria Kew, we decided to put on our work. We'd had a taste of how 'easy' it was with our Trial & Error show, which had included *Killing Rainbows*. By this point, I was eading more playbooks than single plays. *TANK* is clearly influenced by Pinter with its vibe of two men in a room almost talking about nothing. The threat for them is the outcome of their latest audition. *Tick-Tock* bears much credit to Sir Terence Rattigan with its class sensibilities and the outrage over a pregnancy out of wedlock.

During all this time, I was devouring books on writing and attending workshops. I signed up to the intermediate playwriting course at Theatre Royal Bath. This was run by Matt Grinter, who went on to win the Olwen Wymark award for his delivery of it. The final outcome of the course was to have ten minutes of our work, a short play or an excerpt of a longer piece, performed at The Egg. I chose to write a new short piece, *A Game of Two Halves*. It was in part inspired by George Turvey, who suggested that using an event provided a good setting or conclusion to a story. I was pretty familiar with football – a match is often said to be a simile of a play: two halves with an interval – so I used that as the basis for the story but spread it out over a whole season.

The characters of Froggie and Bee both came to life about the same time and to an extent represent human versions of their animal namesakes. The play was cut down to fit the time limit and Chloe Masterton, the director, added the character of a referee to help with both scene changes and the key moment when Froggie is ejected. There is a plan to expand it to full length. On the night, the play was bumped to the end and gathered quite a few laughs. It's much like *TANK* in that it uses the benefit of opposites to examine a theme. In the case of *A Game of Two Halves*, the theme is change. Froggie resists the changes being brought about by the new owners, whereas Bee embraces them.

Chainsaw was written for a good friend, Scott Davenport. He'd been my mentor during the London Screenwriters' Festival's Talent Campus scheme. An advocate for mental health, he put on a night of shorts to raise money and I offered to write a play for it. The play was based on an article I read about the use of AI to scan social media posts to detect people at risk of suicide. One often hears about the more negative aspects of social media and this positive application intrigued me. That didn't stop me putting in the unfortunate ending, but even that is more down to human error than the limitations of the system envisaged.

If short plays are sprints, then full-length plays are marathons. I have something approaching a full-length play, *Midnight Sunrise*, but more work is required to complete it. *Hit Points* came about from the premise of how we treat people with illnesses which are neither visible nor easy to prove clinically. I remember the early scepticism of chronic fatigue syndrome in the eighties and nineties. It was often dismissed as 'yuppie flu'. The phenomenon of benefit cheats also percolated through my mind during its writing. What if someone said they were ill but either couldn't prove it or worse, chose to pretend they were ill in the first place? Why would they do this, and could they be found out? *Hit Points* tries to address these themes.

The final play in this collection is *Loud Mouth*. This play began as an idea several years ago and was inspired somewhat by the film *The Machinist*. I wanted to explore how buried guilt could affect someone. Mashed together with themes of fascism and ageism, the play begins after a world-changing event that has disabled the main character, David. Responsible for a hit-and-run, he appears to be visited by the ghost of the girl he killed. This haunting drives him further and further into a rage against her age group, who he sees as having benefited from the event. The latest edits were focussed on making sure that the apparition could equally be 'real' (in the sense of being physically in the room and a manifestation of Jenny) or a figment of his imagination.

I hope you enjoy reading this collection of plays.

MERLIN GOLDMAN

KILLING RAINBOWS

Killing Rainbows, a Trial & Error production, first presented at the Alma Tavern Theatre from 2–4 June 2016.

It was later performed for one night on 24th October at Bordeaux Quay, with Duncan Bonner in the role of Chris Topley and directed by June Trask as part of a Green Light night. It was then performed at The Room Above in the White Bear on 25th May 2017, directed by Kris Hallett with Tim Whitten in the role.

CAST ///
CHRIS TOPLEY: CHRIS HARRISON

DIRECTED BY /// DANIEL SMITH

CHARACTERS ///
CHRIS TOPLEY: 52 YEARS OLD

SETTING /// BRISTOL

SCENE 1

A man enters in paint-splattered overalls, sweeping the floor.

Chris   I love the smell of Stokes Croft in the morning. It
smells like victory. I came here in the 1980s, to work
as a teacher. I'd been an engineer at the Rover plant
in Birmingham. I'd studied engineering here, my
birthplace, it was meant to be a career for life. It was
honest work, creating an object, working in teams.
But the cars were bland and lacked the soul of those
that built them. Their organs were ugly, twists of
bolted metal. They became generic, each model like
the last, each one sent out to sputter and spew. But
the endeavour was genuine, and the sweat was earnt
through graft. The plant was shut down in the 90s
and the Government sold its remains to corporate
vultures. I returned home. I moved to Stokes Croft,
squatting at first, there was plenty of it. Some took
drugs, some did worse. Many were hopeful and a
few were idealistic, they believed in a better way of
doing things. But it was just talk. I needed to get out.
So, I retrained as a teacher. I taught art to children
who didn't understand its history, its potential

power. I sold some of my own work too on a market stall: slogans in bold palettes. They sold well to students and old socialites. The kids from my class would snicker as they shuffled past. But they were young; I stayed put.

Chris stops sweeping.

SCENE 2

Chris faces the audience.

Chris   How does one make a change? Politics wasn't for me. Politicians deceive us with their rhetoric. They need to be here, with the people, among the grime and pollution. They need to dodge the spitting engines of progress. Metal boxes moving people along concrete lines, separating us from our surroundings. I started small. I bought a shop and sold my artwork. I swept the street outside. I stencilled coloured images on corrugated hoardings. The Council would send men to paint grey squares over them – killing rainbows. I kept painting.

I met my wife at the school, she'd always wanted to be an artist. She taught ICT. She enjoyed my stories about the great artists, their struggles to be heard.

She wanted a better place to live in, she wanted children. I continued to teach, but the other work took more of my time. We sold more artwork, T-shirts and tidied up other streets. Other people started to help out. Another boarded-up shop reopened. The Council stepped up their removal of the 'graffiti' - teams of men were sent out onto our streets in the night. My wife was interviewed by a Community Support Officer about what we were doing. She built a website to share the progress we were making.

This area has always been a vibrant, complex place, on the ley lines of revolution and apathy. I'm much the same, pulled between the 'What's possible?' and 'What pays the bills?' But as people became interested in what we were doing, we noticed a shift. Others began to replicate what we started. Graffiti became street art. Squats became homes. Stokes Croft became a community. I bought this building with the money I made from the shop. My wife wanted an allotment. But it became a mecca for those willing to make things better.

This building is a maze of corridors and odd-shaped rooms. We're in the biggest open space. Upstairs, there'd been a recording studio, and behind me, print artists' studios. This main room was part of the coach works, building carriages for the 'well-to-do'. That's what gives it the height. On the upper floors, they made the leather seats by hand. We hold the bigger events in this room, the others became our offices. We used the studio to make podcasts. This became a factory of art.

It started out small, a few of us, getting together, talking about art, politics and babies. Many I'd met through the market stall or the pubs. Someone told me Banksy was here one night. We told the Council we were a Community Action Group. It gave us the look of authenticity, giving something a name. We even got a couple of grants to tidy up the place, put in some equipment, get broadband throughout. The building became busier. We reached out, further and deeper into the city.

We began with more ambitious artworks on buildings. We sought permission and if none came, we did it anyway. We used some of the slogans I'd created to print more T-shirts. We tidied up any green spaces that had become unloved. We had a radio station. Taken separately, it was a mixed message. Taken together, it was a codex. If you looked hard at each element, you'd not get it. But those that could see through the text, behind the images, they understood the overall message. They self-selected and stayed. And new people started to come along to the meetings. They wanted to believe in something more than material goods and faceless office blocks.

As the numbers grew, the building became full and there were people here all the time. The Council sent in staff to discuss the grants they'd given us. There was an argument, and someone got pushed. The Council refused to make any more payments and threatened to bring in the police. Our website was blocked briefly. I needed to take back some control. So I formed a small group of the most committed, the Godwins, after our idol. You know who E W Godwin is, don't you?

An image of E W Godwin appears behind him.

Chris   Edward William Godwin. He was born in Bristol on the 26th of May 1833. He was a genius. He began his career as an engineer's apprentice and taught himself architecture. He designed the Guildhall in Northampton. He was inspired by Japan and made the most beautiful furniture, ensconced in ebony. Oscar Wilde was one of his clients and Princess Louise, one of Queen Victoria's daughters. He created intricate wallpaper designs: delicate flowers and bold autumn leaves. He designed the front of this building. He was an urban artist - surrounding us with beauty.

The Godwins worked secretly. At first, it was casual, fun stuff, just to see what we could get away with. They did some guerrilla gardening outside Airbus. We closed off streets. We protested outside multinationals trying to open shops in the community. We sent in objections to the Council when developers tried to muscle into the area. We stole materials from construction sites and quarries outside the city. It was minor stuff, but we started to make progress, level the scales.

One morning, after the Godwins had met and dispersed, I met a local woman out on the street. I was cleaning up Turbo Island when she grabbed my arm, pinching my skin. "I know who you are," she said, and "What you're up to." I gripped the broom a little tighter. "I like what you're doing, keep it up. I only wish you'd be a bit quicker – I won't be around forever." The Godwins became more ambitious.

Chris Topley picks up the broom and balances it on his palm.

Chris   Society needs to understand that balance is required. A society is never in balance. It's always swinging between one extreme and the other. Left and right. Rich and poor. Engines of destruction and artistic beauty. But we can't have a society as unbalanced as it is now. Someone has to make a stand. The signs are all around us: the car, the plane, those awful trains. These ugly, oily engines of pollution have become too powerful, tipping the scales. They need to be curbed. We've become blind to the wonder of nature and the environment. We need more art.

Chris drops and catches the broom.

Chris   We started to have more than one meeting a week: two services. We collected money. A few asked what it was for. I didn't have all the answers, but we had to keep going. I told them we could do more. And they did. Some were arrested and some hurt in the increasing confrontations we had. A few suffered chemical burns. But it didn't shake our resolve. More followers came and they kept coming. Social media drove them to our church and the power of the message fuelled their vigour.

On a Sunday morning, the police came to our home. The children cried as I was pushed into the car. In an interview room, they explained what would happen if I failed to stop our activities. They'd close the building and make further arrests. The school would be contacted by the Council, we'd lose our jobs and have to leave the city. The press was waiting outside.

SCENE 3

Chris stands on something to gain height over a crowd in front of him.

Chris   Hello everyone. Thanks for coming. Take a seat if you need to. It's a momentous day. We've all worked so hard to get to this point. We have a community here. Somewhere that is cleaner, colourful and full of kinship. Some have tried to stop us. There have been some that suffered for all of us, and we thank them for their sacrifices. For the Godwins, it's the end of months of hard work, working underground and scaling the sky. You all deserve great credit for the work you've all done.

Our community is strong, and we've reached others online, who've begun their own journey. Today we'll send our message even further and strengthen the resolve of those we've inspired. This will be our greatest work of art. No longer will Brunel be deified and Godwin forgotten. We will bring down this brutal god. Tonight is a celebration of all your hard work. There will be fireworks. So pack up what you can from the building and make your way into the city.

An image of Brunel appears behind him and disintegrates as he speaks.

. **Chris**   When we were all in place, my wife sent the first signal. The traffic was halted. Then she activated the charges. It twisted first one way, then the next. A few cables broke quickly after the first explosion, the others began to scream with the remaining tension. The underground charges laid by the Godwins went next, removing the steel chains' connection to the Earth. The suspension bridge fell first from the Abbot's Leigh side, brushing the cliff face on its descent, metal sparks and branches breaking off, stretching the metal tendons on the other side till they snapped, allowing its body to slump into the canyon's basement. There was a metallic taste on my tongue and the air smelt of burnt oil. Some were too shocked to cheer. Many of the Godwins sank to their knees or clasped each other.

We left in ones and twos, leaving a clear dark canvas, ready for the morning's colour to fill it.

The stage is basked in a rainbow of colour, then fade to black.

OUR KID

Our Kid was written in 2016.

CHARACTERS ///
PRESLEY: MAN, TWENTIES
ELLIOT: MAN, THIRTIES

SETTING ///
A PLAIN ROOM WITH STONE WALLS. THERE
IS A SINGLE HIGH WINDOW. A CHAIR AND
TABLE IN THE MIDDLE.

AUTHOR'S NOTES ///
/ START SPEAKING NEXT LINE

SCENE 1

Yellow light seeps through the window. Presley, dressed in black, drags in Elliot, who is hooded, arms bound behind his back. Presley forces Elliot onto the chair, facing the audience. Presley remains standing and removes Elliot's hood. Elliot is casually dressed in khaki clothing.

Presley   Stay in your seat.

Elliot   Where are we?

Presley   Somewhere hidden. We've got a bit of time to kill before we move on.

Elliot   Where to?

Presley   Just sit there and be quiet.

Elliot   You don't know, do you?

Presley   It's safer that way.

Elliot   Could I have some water?

Presley   No.

Elliot   What's going to happen to me?

Presley   Your fate is with Allah.

Elliot   I don't believe in God. Where are you from?

Presley   Liverpool.

Elliot   Me too. Which part?

Presley   It doesn't matter now.

Elliot   I'm from Fairfield. Are you staying with me?

Presley   Yes. For now.

Elliot   Can I ask some questions?

Presley   For the newspaper?

Elliot   You know I'm a journalist, then?

Presley   Of course. We've been watching you. I've read your articles.

Elliot   What did you think?

Presley   They were okay.

Elliot   It will give an insight into your life here as an ISIS fighter.

Presley   We have other ways of doing that.

Elliot   The Internet.

Presley   Yes.

Elliot   There's a notebook and pen in my pocket. If you untie me, I can take some notes.

Presley   There are others outside. They're armed.

Presley unties Elliot's hands.

Elliot   Thank you. What's your name?

Presley   My Christian name is Presley.

Elliot   That's unusual.

Presley   Yeah, my Dad was into Elvis. He said he met him when he was a kid – I don't believe him. He'd do impersonations all the time – it was embarrassing.

Elliot   I like Elvis.

Presley One Christmas he came in with all the presents
in an Elvis suit and a Father Christmas beard. We
were Muslim – even then it felt wrong.

Elliot Did you get on with your parents?

Presley Not really. I was the oldest. It was always up to
me to toe the line, set an example.

Elliot And that was hard?

Presley Yeah. I had to look after my brothers and sisters
while my parents were working. I didn't get to see
my friends much.

Elliot Did any of your friends come here with you?

Presley No. I lost touch with them when I started going to
the mosque more.

Elliot What's your mother like?

Presley She was strict but she looked after us. She was
always pretty quiet, keeping things tidy round the
house, cooking. She was a good woman, most of
the time.

Elliot What do you mean?

Presley I caught her once.

Elliot Doing what?

Presley I'd been at a meeting at the mosque. Just a
few of us discussing Syria and what the West
was doing. Well, we were walking back and
decided to get some food, so we went down
Stanley Road /

Elliot I know it, there used to be a record shop there,
Heavenly Vinyl, I think. Is it still there?

Presley I don't know. Anyway, it goes past the bingo hall. And there was my mother, with her friends, coming out, laughing.

Elliot She'd been gambling.

Presley She said she met her friends on a Wednesday. Dad used to look after us. But I didn't know she did that.

Elliot Did you confront her?

Presley Not right away. One evening. She said there was nothing wrong with it. She said she didn't buy a bingo card or drink. I said it was still wrong. My dad stepped in, defending her, saying we had to adapt to modern life.

Elliot And what about school – did you enjoy school?

Presley I enjoyed geography and history. I got on with my mates. We mostly supported Liverpool.

Presley shows Elliot the red Liverpool FC band around his wrist.

Elliot I'm an Everton fan. I went to Goodison a few times. I saw Beardsley and Linker play. My first game was a derby match for my birthday. We arrived slightly late. I remember climbing up the steps to the terrace – the noise was incredible. All those people, sitting in their tribal colours, chanting together.

Presley I never went to a game – it was too expensive. But we used to bunk off school sometimes. Head down

to the club store. My mates would spend all their
money on shirts and stuff.

Elliot You didn't approve?

Presley I didn't mind at the time. But I know it's wrong
now. This desire to own more and more things.
Muhammad tells the story of three ancient
peoples. The leaders get involved in a contest,
competing with each other. They discuss how
many possessions they have, the strength of
their armies and their spoils of war. They keep
trying to outdo each other. They start more
wars, take more wives, steal more possessions.
They argue over and over who has killed the
most, to determine who should be the supreme
ruler. To settle the debate, they open up all
the graves and dig up the dead, piling them
up. They begin to count. They start at sunrise
and continue all the way into the evening. The
smell is putrid, and the air becomes thick with
flies, but they keep counting. As they are doing
so, a Holy Prophet arrives. He is disgusted at
their behaviour. He stops them and orders them
to rebury the dead. The three leaders fall to
their knees in front of him, ashamed. He says
to them, "He who values possessions shall
not enter heaven, for only the man that leaves
this world empty-handed as a destitute will be
allowed in."

Elliot   I've read some of the Quran. Do you read it a lot?

Presley   Every day.

Elliot   What about the Internet – did you use that at all before you came here?

Presley   Yeah, we use it here too – to get the message out. You can find the truth on there, hidden from view.

Elliot   Did it influence your decision to come here?

Presley   It told me stuff they don't show on TV. What's really going on. Videos of holy men, explaining things.

Elliot   Do you miss home? Liverpool. I moved away but I go back to see my parents.

Presley   This is my home now. I prefer it.

Elliot   Why?

Presley   The people – they're pure. They'll do anything for you. We believe in something. Not just getting drunk or chatting up girls.

Elliot   You don't approve of a man dating several women before he finds the right one?

Presley   No.

Adhan – call to prayer – can be heard. They both stop to listen.

Elliot   I used to go to church on a Sunday with my parents when I was a kid. The bells sounded so mournful – I hated it. They'd pull me along so hard, the fronts of my shoes would scuff against the pavement. They'd get even angrier.

Afterwards, we'd go for Sunday lunch. My mother would always give me her Yorkshire pudding. And before we went my father would let me push the buttons on the fruit machine. "Quick, nudge down!" he'd say. And if we won, he'd give me a one pound coin. I used to pretend it was a gold coin from a treasure chest.

Presley   I'll need to go now.

He reties Elliot's arms to the chair, then exits. Elliot struggles with the ropes and manages to get himself free.

Elliot   Okay, now what?

Elliot gets up and walks around the room, looking inquisitively. Presley's voice is heard from outside. Elliot considers picking up the chair as a weapon, but sits back down. Presley enters the room with a cup.

Presley   Would you like some water? It's not fresh but it's all we've got.

Elliot   Yes.

Presley lifts it to Elliot's mouth. He drinks some water without using his hands.

Elliot   Thank you – it's hot.

Presley   Yes, not like Liverpool – always cloudy.

Elliot As a kid I'd go out on my bike with my friends to the Pier Head. During the winter, the fog would be so thick, only the top of the Liver Birds was visible. One morning, we heard this screeching noise coming from the Mersey. We couldn't see what was causing it and the fog had completely covered the statues. One of my friends shouted, "They've come to life!". We got really spooked and sped off in hysterics. It took weeks before we cycled that way again. (*Pause*) Do you miss anything about home?

Presley No. Things have gone too far back in England. The materialism makes me sick. And the women, the way they behave. I used to go to early morning prayers. I'd see these girls coming back from clubs or walking alone back from some guy's house, half-dressed. It's not decent – it's an obscenity.

Elliot But they were not knowingly trying to insult your religion. They were living to their own moral code. They will not even be aware of the Quran and what it says about how women should dress.

Presley It doesn't matter. All deviants must be punished.

Elliot Do you not think religions should adapt to the modern day?

Presley No. "Every change is a misguidance, and every misguidance is going astray and every astray is in the hell-fire." (*Pause*) Do you want any more water?

Elliot   No, I'm fine, thank you.

Presley goes to leave stage left with the cup but turns to check Elliot's bindings.

Presley   They seem to have come loose.
Elliot   Why don't you leave them like that? I'm not planning an escape. I'd like to make some notes.
Presley   Look, I'll tie your hands together but not to the chair. So you can still write. Do you have much more to do?
Elliot   Not much.

The sound of a helicopter can be heard. Then gunfire. Presley goes to the window and looks out.

Elliot   What's happening?
Presley   It looks like someone may be trying to find you.

An explosion is heard. Lights go out. Lights come back on. Elliot is standing.

Elliot   Jesus.
Presley   Sit down!

Presley ties Elliot to the chair, then runs out. More gunfire is heard before silence. Night falls. The light changes from yellow to blue. Elliot falls asleep, head on the table.

Vegas–style lights appear. Presley appears dressed as a jihadi Elvis and dances to the tune of Elvis Presley's 'I don't wanna be tied'. Only a minute or so is required.

Lights fade. Presley leaves stage left. Orange–red daylight emerges through the window. The call to prayer can be heard. Elliot wakes up, realises he is still bound. Presley returns to the stage in full jihadist clothing, brandishing a knife.

Elliot   What happened?

Presley   They came for you. They killed some of my brothers. We killed many of them.

Elliot   Are they all dead?

Presley   Several of them are still alive.

Elliot   Why don't you let me go, then you could escape?

Presley   There is no escape from the will of God. Non-believers must be punished.

Elliot   Make sure my notes reach home.

Lights fade. A TV–like spotlight on Elliot with Presley behind him.

Elliot   My name is Elliot. I'm a journalist from Liverpool. I've been given some words to say. But before I do, I'd like to quote something from a song:

Don't be afraid of the dark.
At the end of a storm is a golden sky
And the sweet silver song of a lark.

Walk on, walk on with hope in your heart
And you'll never walk alone,
You'll never, ever walk alone.

Presley brings the knife in front of Elliot's neck. Lights out.

TICK-TOCK

Tick-Tock was a co-production by Space Opera Theatre and Magnetical and was presented as an evening of shorts under the moniker Pantomime Shorts. It was performed at the Alma Tavern Theatre from 3–8 January in 2017, along with *TANK, Double Trouble* by Euphoria Kew and *Little Red Riding Hoodie* by Stuart Smith.

CAST ///
NICK: DANIEL ECCLESTON
ALISON: MEG PICKUP
JENNY: IMOGEN GREENWOOD
BILL: BEN NASH

DIRECTED BY /// DANIEL SMITH
LIGHTING AND SOUND BY /// SYNOLDA ROSS

CHARACTERS ///

NICK STATION:	56 YEARS OLD, AMERICAN ACTOR, PLAYING HOOK
ALISON FINCH:	49 YEARS OLD, ENGLISH STAGE MANAGER
JENNY FINCH:	25 YEARS OLD, ENGLISH UNDERSTUDY, ALISON'S DAUGHTER
BILL THURROCK:	62 YEARS OLD, SCOTTISH PRODUCER

SETTING ///
A PROVINCIAL THEATRE'S DRESSING ROOM. THERE IS A GENERAL BUSTLE TO PROCEEDINGS PRIOR TO THE FIRST NIGHT'S PERFORMANCE OF *PETER PAN*.

AUTHOR'S NOTES ///
/ START SPEAKING NEXT LINE

SCENE 1

Alison Finch is in the dressing room checking the costumes and props. Bill enters holding a tabloid newspaper.

Bill   Ali. Thank God. You need to phone your daughter.

Alison   I'm not sure where she is.

Bill   Michelle Bachelor has pulled out - we need a new Peter Pan.

Alison   It's opening night, for heaven's sake.

Bill   It's the best time to release a story like this. Our wee soap star's been having an affair with a member of the shadow cabinet.

Alison   That makes a change from footballers.

Bill   Can you phone Jenny - get her in as soon as possible?

Alison   She's not rehearsed once with the cast. Can't you find someone else? I really don't think it's a good idea.

Bill   Why not?

Alison   She's not very well.

Bill   Oh dear, I'm sorry to hear that. I'm sure a few aspirin can get her through it. It's too late to find someone else. This could be the big break she's been looking for.

Alison   I know and I really appreciate you getting her involved. But she's been suffering from anxiety attacks. On bad days, she can't leave the house.

Bill   You should have told me. I remember Dance in *The Taming of the Shrew* in seventy-two. He wouldn't leave his dressing room. The SM was banging on the door - he wouldn't budge. I told him I had a bottle of Tobermory - I knew it was his favourite. A wee dram and an arm round the shoulder was all he needed. The papers called it a "tour de force." I hadn't realised it had come back.

Alison   It never really went away.

Bill   But this is a good opportunity - she shouldn't miss out on this.

Alison   Panto?

Bill   Some of the greats started in pantomime. I remember Rylance in Margate in seventy-nine. He played Buttons; he was quite / superb.

Alison   I really appreciate it. I'll give her a call.

Bill   Thanks, dear. Break a leg!

Bill turns to leave.

Alison   Wait, Bill, there's something else.

Bill   What is it, dear?

Alison   Do you remember I told you about the American actor who'd come here after RADA?

Bill   I don't recall.

Alison   He was in a Pinter play.

Bill   No, still nothing.

Alison   The night on the beach.

Bill   Jenny.

Alison   Yes, Jenny.

Bill   She'll get to work opposite a great actor.

Alison   But that's her father.

Bill   And he still doesn't know?

Alison   I never thought I'd see him again. He comes to the UK if he's got a film to promote, but that's always in London. I can't have Jenny here, with him.

Bill   Why not?

Alison   It would feel deceitful.

Bill   After twenty years?

Alison   But I've not had to think about it in all that time, except since...

Alison's upset.

Bill I know it's still raw, don't upset yourself.

Alison We never spoke about it when he was alive.

Bill Roger was a decent man, but she has the right to know. So does Nick Station for that matter.

Alison He left. He played his part. He doesn't deserve an encore.

Bill Maybe not, but doesn't Jenny still deserve this chance?

Bill leaves. Alison phones her daughter. Nick enters. Alison is not immediately aware of him.

Alison Jenny. (*Pause*) Look, you're needed tonight. (*Pause*) You saw the papers. (*Pause*) She's pulled out, you'll need to come in. (*Pause*) Yes, I know you're not feeling well but this is a great opportunity. (*Pause*) Not all Americans are full of themselves. (*Pause*) Yes, now, get a taxi if you have to. (*Pause*) Bye.

Nick Hi, is this mine?

Alison tries to hide her face.

Alison Yes. No. You have your own, next door.

Nick Stage manager, right? Alison Parrot, isn't it? I'm Nick. Nick Station.

Nick holds out a hand. Alison responds weakly.

Alison   It's Finch.

Nick   I knew it was something avian. Have we met?

Alison   I'd remember if we did.

Nick   Are you sure? I'm clearly not very good with names. But faces, faces I never forget.

Alison   I bet you've seen a lot of faces.

Nick   Don't believe everything you read. Most of my *girlfriends* were fake – part of the PR machine. Finding someone genuine in Hollywood ain't easy.

Alison   I'm sure you had fun trying. Well, you don't get much closer to real life than pantomime in a coastal town that's seen better days.

Nick   I like it. Or I did. I've been here before. Everyone was so friendly. British actors are still the best I've ever worked with. I'd just graduated from RADA; I was in a Pinter play here prior to it moving to the West End.

Alison   You were very good, or so I heard.

Nick   Are you sure we haven't met?

Alison   Did you hear that Michelle has pulled out?

Nick   It's a damn pity, the rehearsals in London had gone great. It's not enough that politicians lie their way into government, put there by money men we've never seen. Once in power, they're corrupted by it and cheat us all. He was married as well. Jeez.

Alison   Roger was always faithful. (*Beat*) My daughter Jenny will be playing Peter Pan now.

Nick	I look forward to meeting her. Where did she study?
Alison	Bolton School of Dramatic Arts.
Nick	You said my room was next door.
Alison	Just on the right.

Nick goes to leave.

Alison	Nick.
Nick	Yes.
Alison	If you need anything, just ask.

Nick leaves. Alison paces about the room, trying to be useful. Stops and starts to cry. Jenny enters.

Jenny	Hi, Mom.
Alison	Hello, dear.
Jenny	Are you okay?
Alison	I'm fine. Did you get a taxi?
Jenny	It was ten pounds.
Alison	I'll give it to you later. How are you with your lines?
Jenny	It's only panto – no one will notice if I screw up.
Alison	Nick might?
Jenny	Who?
Alison	Your...Hook.
Jenny	The *film star*. Do you think he realises we don't do retakes?

Alison   Be professional, Jenny, you'll be opposite a well-known actor. Remember what happened at / your RADA audition.

Jenny   Okay - don't keep going on about it. Bolton was good enough, it's the same course. I don't need some trumped-up school to make me a good actor. So where is the mighty 'Bounty Hunter'?

Alison   Don't call him that - he's in his dressing room. He went to RADA.

Jenny   And what did he do with it? Some stupid TV show where he chased baddies in a red pick-up truck.

Alison   It ran for six series.

Jenny   He's a has-been. He's just here for the money.

Alison   Money's not an evil in itself. If it wasn't for Roger doing so much overtime, we'd have really struggled when you were a child.

Jenny picks up the Peter Pan costume.

Alison   Now, is Michelle's costume going to be okay for you? You've been putting on a bit of weight lately.

Jenny   At least I've not been starving myself like that bloody soap reject.

Alison   A little less might not be such / a bad thing.

Jenny   Mother.

Alison   There's something I want to talk to you about. Do you remember when we had that chat with

Roger about why you didn't have any brothers
or sisters?

Jenny   Low sperm count, do we have to?

Alison   Not that. About your father?

Jenny   Dad's dead.

Alison   Your biological father.

Jenny   Dad was my father. That's all that matters.

Alison   Yes, he was, and we said we'd never talk about
it while he was alive. But he's not here any more
and there's things you need to know.

Jenny   It's only been six months.

Alison   Seven.

Jenny   What more do I need to know – what does it
matter now?

Alison   Well, sometimes it's not the right time to talk
about something. Other times it is. I think this is
the right moment to tell you what happened.

Bill comes into the room.

Bill   Ali, Nick needs some adjustments to his
costume. His hook is loose. Can you go in
and have a look?

Alison   (*To Jenny*) We'll speak about this later.

Alison leaves.

Bill   Hello, Jenny, how are you feeling?

Jenny   I'm fine. Perfect. It's a shame about
what's-her-face. Ticket sales will be affected.

Bill   We've still got Nick Station.

Jenny   That overpaid Yank.

Bill   Yes, well, anyway. He seems like a decent chap.
Strong opinion on politics. Reminds me of you in
a funny sort of way.

Jenny   That's not funny.

Bill   No, no, actually it's not. Forget I said anything.
Anyway, it can't be helped now. The story will
be chip paper in the morning. I'm so pleased you
could step in at short notice. I know it's not the
sort of role you're looking for, but you have to
start somewhere. I remember seeing Branagh in
Henry V in eighty-four. He was superb, he had the
audience / in the palm of his hand.

Jenny   Thank you for the opportunity, Bill, really, it
means a lot to know you're looking out for us.

Bill   I saw all your school plays.

Jenny   Did you? I didn't know you were there.

Bill   Your mum thought it was best I stayed out of
sight. With your dad and all.

Jenny   What did you think?

Bill   You showed promise. Definitely. Right, I'd
better head off - see how many returns we have
for tonight.

Bill leaves.

Jenny   Hold on, what do you mean, "promise"?

Nick enters.

Nick   Is Alison in here? This hook is still not right.

Jenny   No, she's not.

Nick   So, you're the new Pan?

Jenny   And you're the old Hook?

Nick   What is it about your British politicians? They just can't keep their pants on.

Jenny   I don't think yours are much better.

Nick   That's true – but who could have resisted Marilyn? And what an actress. Have you been in any movies?

Jenny   I want to be a stage actress, it's the higher art form.

Nick   All the best roles go to movie stars now.

Jenny   Which is demeaning to stage actors, who've worked hard. We go to auditions knowing full well that some C-list celebrity will take the lead role.

Nick   I realised long ago that it's okay to be angry with the system, but there's no point fighting against it unless you think you can win. Without it, I wouldn't be here.

Jenny   Here. Here. This is pantomime in a crummy seaside theatre. Why would you want to be here?

Nick   Places hold memories. But more than that, they trigger feelings. If I hear the name of somewhere I've been, I get an emotional response, even if I don't remember why I've been there. My British agent made me the offer thinking I'd refuse. But when he told me where it was, I knew I had to agree to it because of the feeling it gave me. Like footprints in the sand, fading but still beautiful. I stayed in a little guest house around the corner. It was on Potter Street... or was it Parsons Street?

Jenny   Parsons Street. We're two streets further down.

Nick   The owner had this little dog - it would attack me every time I came back from rehearsals. I found if I gave it a chip, I could sneak past before it got its teeth into me. I tried fish and chips for the first time here, on a beach. Do they still do that here?

Jenny   Yes, it really caught on. I expect you're more used to eating sushi nowadays.

Nick   We can get everything in LA. Even fish and chips, although I've never tried them there yet. We should go for fish and chips after the show.

Jenny   If you're paying. The money's not so good when you're performing in profit-share pieces to half a dozen of your friends above a pub. Not all of us get whisked off to Hollywood after one run.

Nick   Why don't you try TV?

Jenny   You make it sound so easy.

Nick   I could make a few calls. You're beautiful, the camera would love you.

Jenny Do you think so? My mother says I'm fat.

Nick Let me look at you.

Nick grabs Jenny by the waist and looks her up and down.

Nick You've got a good figure.

Jenny pulls away.

Jenny Should we go over the lines?

Nick We can if you want to. Or we could let the excitement of the opening night carry us through. I have a feeling we're going to be a good match.

Jenny Don't forget, I'm your sworn enemy. I'm pretty handy with a sword.

Nick But it's the crocodile that gets me in the end. Time catches up with all of us. Just like the Californian sun on my skin.

Jenny You're not looking so bad. You studied at RADA – what was it like? Full of pretentious wannabes, I bet.

Nick Awesome. There was so much talent there. It was intimidating.

Jenny For you - the great 'Bounty Hunter'?

Nick I did my own stunts until I broke my pelvis. I've not felt it in years, but it's quite stiff today.

Jenny That's because it's so damp here. My father had rheumatism in his knees - he always felt it in winter. Part of the pier collapsed into the sea last year – you better watch out.

Nick Let's hope that doesn't happen. Is your father not around?

Jenny No, he's dead.

Nick I'm sorry.

Jenny I wanted to go to RADA, but I didn't make it to the interview.

Nick These things happen, I've missed several auditions after being canned / the night before.

Jenny I had a panic attack. I have them for anything that makes me stressed. I nearly didn't make it here. If I'd had more time to think about it, you'd have been fighting yourself.

Nick When did they start?

Jenny I don't know for certain. I had a few when I was a teenager, but when my father got ill they became more frequent.

Nick What was he like?

Jenny Kind. Quiet. He didn't understand acting or what Mum does, but he supported us. If it wasn't for him, I might not have gone into acting.

Nick My father sent me here. He hoped I'd be a great stage actor, like him. When I told him what I was coming back to do...well, we never really spoke again. He said I was wasting my talent.

Jenny My mother's seen every episode of *The Bounty Hunter*. Even that pilot you did.

Nick   *Space Station 9.*

Jenny   I thought it was funny.

Nick   It wasn't meant to be.

Jenny   I remember that bit when the alien slug thing
             started sucking on your face. I couldn't stop
             giggling – my mother was really upset.

Nick   I didn't get a lot of work after that.

Jenny   Do you really think I could make it in TV?

Nick moves towards Jenny so that they are face to face.

Nick   I think you've got the perfect face to be sucked on
             by an alien slug monster.

Alison comes in. Nick and Jenny separate.

Alison   Bill says you're still having trouble with that
             hook.

Nick   It's not tight enough.

Jenny   It felt okay to me.

Alison   Let me have a look at it. (*To Jenny*) Jenny, have
             you made sure they've updated the website with
             your name?

Jenny   Not yet.

Alison   Go and do it now.

Jenny   Fine.

Jenny exits. Alison looks at the hook.

Nick   Cute girl.

Alison   She's put on some weight lately. And she's got a temper on her too – lost many a role because of it.

Nick   She's young, she'll grow out of it. I did. Women used to like that about me. Some still do. Does she have a boyfriend?

Alison   She's my daughter.

Nick   I can see the resemblance. An attractive woman.

Alison   Yes, she is. (*Pause*) Oh, you mean me.

Nick   When were you going to tell me?

Alison   Tell you what?

Nick   That we'd met before.

Alison   I didn't think you'd remember. It was a long time ago.

Nick   We had fish and chips on the beach at midnight. And we made love in the sand dunes.

Alison   I remember the 'And'.

Nick   How have you been?

Alison   Good. Very good, in fact. I've been happy. I know this isn't California, but we have the sea too.

Nick   You still have fish and chips.

Alison   We do. How's the life of a celebrity?

Nick   Everything I expected. Money, fast cars and girls.

Alison   Did they make you happy?

Nick   Often. But sometimes when you get everything you want, you realise it's not what you need.

Alison   I got married.

Nick   Jenny said he died – was it recent?

Alison   Seven months.

Nick   I'm sorry.

Alison   Don't be, we were happy – he was ill for a long
time. In the end, it was a blessing. He was in
a lot of pain. When Jenny was a child and I
was working, he looked after her. He never
complained. She had the main role in all her
school plays – she can be really good when she
puts her mind to it. (*Pause*) Would you help her?
She's desperate to move on to better roles.

Nick   My British agent should be here soon – I'll talk to
her. Jenny could come to California. She could stay
with me.

Alison   She's not a very good traveller, I don't think she
would be able to get on the plane. But thanks for
the offer about your agent. I think I've fixed it.

Alison hands Nick the hook.

Nick   I'd better get my make-up done.

Nick goes to exit.

Alison   That night on the beach. You said the moon was
making the waves just for us. Did you / mean it?

Bill sticks his head in.

Bill   *The Courier* are in. Could you come out and do some interviews, Nick? Just go through to the foyer, your agent is there with our press officer.

Nick   Sure thing, William.

Nick leaves. Bill enters. Alison is tearful.

Bill   Are you okay, Alison?

Alison   I don't know what's wrong with me today. I seem to be all over the place. Since Roger died, I seem to cry at the slightest thing. I burst into tears last week when the bin bag broke.

Bill hands her his handkerchief.

Bill   That's okay, I remember how it is. It's like a tap with a worn washer, it's never completely shut – always ready to rush out. When I lost Philip, I thought I'd never be the same. And I wasn't. Why should you be when you've lost the love of your life? But that doesn't mean it doesn't get easier.

Alison   I'll be fine. It seems / that...

Bill starts to cry.

Bill   You've set me off now.

Alison   I'm sorry, Bill.

Alison embraces Bill. Jenny comes in.

Jenny   I knew it – it's him!

Alison   It's not what you think.

Jenny   Don't lie to me. He's the sperm donor!

Bill   What?

Alison   Don't be silly, Jenny.

Jenny   Don't try to shut me up. It was him, wasn't it?
He's my father. I should have guessed, always
turning up at birthdays and such. Well, I think it's
despicable. Being around all of my childhood and
keeping it a secret.

Bill   I can tell you, Jenny, I am not your father. I am
not anyone's father, and never will I be.

Jenny   I want a DNA test.

Alison   Now, Jenny, don't be silly. You're on stage in a
couple of hours. Don't go working yourself up like
this – you know what happens?

Jenny   I lose it, that's what you're saying, aren't you? Just
like RADA and all the other ones. If it wasn't for
someone you knew, I'd have never got into Bolton.

Alison   Well, we were lucky we knew someone who
knew someone.

Jenny   It was you wasn't it? (*Looking at Bill*)

Bill   I don't know what to say.

Alison   You can tell her.

Bill   It was me. Or more it was a friend of mine.

Jenny   A friend. What friend?

Alison	Now, you don't need to know the details.
Jenny	I want to know.
Bill	It was / the
Alison	You don't need to tell her.
Bill	It's quite all right, Ali. I used to work up there and attend...certain clubs. I got to know a young fellow quite well and we stayed in touch. For quite a while, in fact, until he had children. It just so happens he's married to the admissions tutor.
Jenny	I remember her - she used to scowl at me every time I walked past her office.
Bill	She wasn't too keen on bending the rules.
Jenny	I'm sure I would have got in somewhere eventually. But thank you.
Alison	Bill has always looked out for you, but he's not your father.
Jenny	Then who is?
Alison	You've never wanted to know before. You said Roger was your father and it didn't matter.
Jenny	It does now. I don't know why, but it does.
Alison	It's not easy to tell you.

Nick enters.

Jenny	Just tell me who my father is!?
Nick	Hey, is this a warm-up exercise - can I join in?
Bill	I think I'll be off.
Alison	You should stay, Bill.

Jenny   He knows?

Bill   I was sworn to secrecy, Jenny, I'm awfully sorry.

Nick   Sorry to interrupt, but the press officer wants to see you, William. He's says it's something about Michelle Bachelor.

Bill   I'd better go.

Bill hurries from the room.

Alison   It was my fault. I needed to confide in someone. I couldn't speak about it to Roger – he didn't want to know. He loved you so much, Jenny, and he will always be your father. As for the 'sperm donor' – well, it was never going to work out.

Jenny   Why?

Alison   He wouldn't have been interested. I knew it was just a holiday romance. He was going to get on a plane and go back to his old life.

Nick   How do you know he wouldn't have stayed? You never asked him.

Alison   I just knew. Fish and chips are a lovely treat, but it's not something you have every day.

Nick   You're right – I wasn't mature enough to handle something like that.

Jenny   You?

Nick   I think so.

Alison   Yes, him.

Jenny   Oh, shit.

Alison   Nick's offered to help you out with some contacts
         here and in the States. I told him you don't
         like flying.

Jenny   Do you have a pool?

Nick   Yes.

Jenny   Is it heated?

Nick   Sometimes – usually it's so hot we don't need to.

Jenny   I want to go. Oh my God – you're my dad. I mean,
         not my real dad. My 'sperm donor'. I can't call you
         that. I'll need to think of another name. America,
         I've never been there. Mother, how could you not
         have told me when you knew how famous he was?

Alison   You said TV acting wasn't real / acting.

Jenny   I'm sure I didn't. When can I go? I'll have to
         buy more clothes. For auditions. And going out.
         Mother, you'll need to lend me some money.

Alison   Calm down, Jenny – you're on stage soon. Try to
         keep calm.

Bill enters the room.

Bill   Can I come in?

Alison   Yes, it's okay, Bill, come in. They both know.

Bill   I'm afraid I have some bad news, Jenny. Michelle
         Bachelor has decided to come back to the show.
         Her agent told me she's quite enjoying the extra
         publicity. On top of that, her autobiography is due
         out next week.

Jenny	She's twenty-eight.
Bill	That's as may be, but they want to keep her profile as high as possible.
Jenny	Media whore.
Alison	That's enough, Jenny. There'll be other opportunities.
Bill	Yes, I'm sure there will be. Our next show is a musical and it has one or two good female supporting roles.
Jenny	I think I'll try TV.
Nick	We'll still have one night together.
Jenny	And fish and chips.
Alison	I think I'm going to cry again.
Bill	It reminds me of the time I saw Jackson in *Ophelia* in / sixty-seven.
All but Bill	Oh, shut up!

Lights out.

TANK

TANK was a co-production by Space Opera Theatre and Magnetical and was presented as an evening of shorts under the moniker Pantomime Shorts. It was performed at the Alma Tavern Theatre from 3–8 January in 2017, along with *Tick-Tock, Double Trouble* by Euphoria Kew and *Little Red Riding Hoodie* by Stuart Smith.

CAST ///
FRONT: DANIEL ECCLESTON
BACK: BEN NASH

CHARACTERS ///
FRONT: AN ADULT
BACK: AN ADULT

SETTING ///
A MOSTLY BARE STORAGE OR DRESSING ROOM NEXT TO A LARGER ROOM BEING USED AS AN AUDITION SPACE. A SINGLE BENCH OR TWO CHAIRS.

SCENE 1

Front and Back enter wearing two halves of a pantomime horse costume. They are sweaty. Front carries the head.

Front   This is empty, let's wait here.

Back   Do you think we got it?

Front   I hope so.

Back   The judges were pretty stern.

Front   That's how they normally are.

Back   I'm thirsty – it was warm in there.

Front   I left the water in the audition space, sorry, along with our music. Shall I go and get it?

Back   Don't worry, I'll be okay, we'll get them when they've finished.

Front   Has your father said when we'll get the loan?

Back   No, not yet. He's got a lot on his mind. (*Beat*) How do you think we did?

Front   I know we need to get this one. If we don't, I think we should pack it in. It's just too expensive attending all these auditions but not getting the part. Especially now as we're saving for the house.

Back   But you love doing this.

Front I do, but sometimes you have to know when you're not good enough at something and move on.

Back You think I messed up again, don't you?

Front I wouldn't know – you're always behind me.

Back That doesn't mean I always want to be. I think it went quite well.

Front You kicked left when you should have kicked right.

Back So you did know! Why didn't you say anything?

Front I didn't want to upset you – you know how you are?

Back No, how am I?

Front You'll get upset.

Back I'll get upset when you tell me how I get upset?

Front Yes.

Back Tell me anyway.

Front You get all sullen and you start mumbling. You curl your lower lip.

Back Mumbling?

Front Yes. Mumbling. No one can hear you.

Back Maybe they're not listening.

Front What do you mean by that?

Back You don't listen to my suggestions. We always do what you want to do.

Front Like this. This is how you get.

Back Well, you should still tell me, even if whatever it is will upset me.

Front I like it when you curl your lip. It's cute.

Back Like this?

Back curls lip.

Front Stop it.

Back Do you trust me?

Front I do trust you. Most of the time. Have you spoken to your dad?

Back Not yet – I'll do it soon.

Front You said that last week. This is why I don't trust you.

Back Some of the time. You said you trust me most of the time.

Front Yes, but I don't know when that will be. You say you will do things and I don't know whether this will be the time you will do it. You say you want to live together, but how do I know you mean it?

Back It's a big step.

Front We spend most weekends together already. We've been on holiday at least twice.

Back This is different. This is a proper grown-up thing to do. This is sharing the bills, not using up all the milk, major stuff.

Front It used to make me so mad when my brother and sister did that.

Back What did you do?

Front I'd make them go in the garden. Then I'd lock the doors. Once, I completely forgot about them. It rained and they got completely soaked. They'd been banging on the windows for ages. I was upstairs on the PS – didn't hear a thing.

Back   Would you do that to me?

Front   We might not have a garden; I'd have to use the attic. So will you ask him?

Back   I will. I promise.

Front   Interest rates are really low at the moment.

Back   Can it have a garden?

Front   Yes, if you want it to.

Back   And a pond.

Front   Yes, if it doesn't have one.

Back   I like fish. I never had them as a kid, although I always wanted to. My mother wouldn't let me. She said she'd only end up having to feed them. (*Pause*) I'm afraid.

Front   Of ponds?

Back   It's hard to explain. There will be so many things to sort out. I know most of them are small things. But it's as if they are sticking to me one by one until I'm completely covered so I can't move or breathe. Like those plant things.

Front   Burrs.

Back   What?

Front   They're called burs. It's a seed or fruit with hooks.

Back   Okay, Attenborough. Why do they do that?

Front   To get somewhere new usually. It will be great to have our own place. We just need some cash to help with the deposit.

Back   There'll be so much to sort out.

Front   And we'll deal with each, one by one.

Back I'm sorry, but I've always been anxious about these types of things. That's why I like the costume.

Front This flimsy thing?

Back Not to me. To me, it's like a tank. It makes me feel safe when I'm inside it. I can think anything, be anyone, go anywhere.

Front Anywhere?

Back I know people are watching, but it's like they're watching a different version of me. A stronger, more confident version.

Front You should have told me.

Back When I was a kid, if I got scared or someone was mean to me, I'd hide under the duvet. I'd pretend I was some sort of bug, waiting to hatch. And when I was ready, I'd emerge as something bigger and stronger. I opened my GCSE and A level results that way.

Front You got good grades.

Back That doesn't mean I don't still get scared sometimes. Especially of doing something I've not done before.

Front Whenever I suggest new things to do, you always agree.

Back I'm still scared but I trust you to make good choices. Most of the time.

Front Are you scared of me?

Back When you shout at me.

Front I don't, do I? I don't mean to.

Back When you raise your voice, it feels like you're telling me what to do.

Front I don't mean to boss you about but when you don't say anything, I assume you're happy to go along with things. When my mother started dating again, she left me in charge. When not locked out of the house, my brother and sister were a real handful. I had to learn how to take control. (*Pause*) I never knew you felt that way.

Back I hid it. I was embarrassed.

Front We'll be living together soon – hiding under the duvet won't be an option. If you're scared of doing something, I can always do it for you.

Back But I don't want you to do everything for me.

Front But if it's making you nervous. I enjoy doing things for you.

Back But I can do it. It just takes me a little bit of time to build up to it.

Front When will your dad give us the money?

Back I've not asked him.

Front What! You promised.

Back I've been worried about the audition – I know how important it is to you. And I had to make repairs to the costume.

Front This is why I don't trust you.

Back Some of the time.

Front Most of the time. Remember that time you said you'd book the accommodation for our weekend in Bognor Regis?

Back　That was ages ago.

Front　But still, you said you'd book somewhere.

Back　We got something in the end.

Front　But I had to book it.

Back　I hope we don't go there again – there wasn't a lot to see.

Front　We made the best of it.

Back　If a room above a biker's disco and the model village is your idea of a romantic break.

Front　If you'd booked the accommodation when I asked you, we would have been someone better.

Back　I did mean to do it, I just got distracted. And you normally do that sort of thing.

Front　But you wanted to do it – so you could pick something that you liked.

Back　I just needed more time. I like to take a run-up to these sorts of things. I can't do things as quickly as you.

Front　Why don't you call him now?

Back　Now?

Front　We're not doing anything.

Back　I was going to do it this weekend when I go and visit.

Front　That sounds like you're putting it off.

Back　What if he says no?

Front　He won't, will he – not for you, his only child. Go on, give him a call.

Back　On one condition.

Front　Sure.

Back   That I can wear it?

Front   What?

Back   The head.

Front   To make a phone call?

Back   It will make it easier.

Front   It's been specially fitted for me.

Back   Please.

Front   Okay.

Front helps to put the head on Back. Back takes it back off.

Back   You have got a funny-shaped head, haven't you?

Front pushes the head on Back, holding their phone. We see head movements. Front walks around. Back takes off the head.

Front   What did he say?

Back   He wasn't in.

Front   Who were you talking to, then?

Back   Mother.

Front   What did she say?

Back   She said the neighbours refused to cut down their leylandii.

Front   About the loan!

Back   I didn't ask her about it.

Front   Why not?

Back   Because we're asking my dad.

Front   You're unbelievable. How is she?

Back   She's feeling okay. She said we can ask him this weekend. Over Sunday lunch. Do you want to come?

Front   If you want me to.

Back   You don't normally want to come.

Front   I've never said that.

Back   You say it's too stuffy.

Front   It's too hot – that's different.

Back   So do you want to come?

Front   There's football on the television, but if you need me to ask them with you.

Back   I don't need you to. That's not why I'm asking you.

Front   So why are you asking?

Back   Because we're a couple and we do things together.

Front   Like living together.

Back   Eventually. So, are you coming with me?

Front   It doesn't sound like you want me to. I'll watch the football.

Back   Fine, don't come.

Front   Don't forget to ask him when we'll get the loan.

Back   What did you think about the turn in the middle – could it have gone better?

Front   We should be smoother by now. Chris picked it up much quicker.

Back   Is he back at work?

Front   No, no – he's still laid up at home.

Back   So, you're speaking again?

Front   I sent him a text.

Back   He's still not forgiven you.

Front   I told him to watch out for the edge of the stage on the last turn.

Back   I bet they've never seen a horse split in two like that before.

Front   I never told you that the stage manager fainted when she saw his broken leg.

Back   Really?!

Front   When the paramedics arrived, they didn't know which one of them to treat first. Chris was surprisingly calm. When I told him he'd never be better in time for this year's pantomime season, all the colour seemed to return to his face. Luckily enough, you agreed.

Back   Yes, lucky. Did I have much of a choice?

Front   Of course you did, but I knew you wouldn't let me down. At least not about this.

Back   What does that mean?

Front   Because we're doing this together, I can keep an eye on you.

Back   I thought you said you couldn't see me. (*Beat*) Do you think they've made a decision yet?

Front   It shouldn't be much longer.

Back   Why don't you go and check?

Front   But you could...never mind.

Front goes and checks, then returns.

Front   They've still got one more to audition.

Back   Who is it?

Front   Geoff and Linda.

Back   You said they're the best – we've got no chance, then.

Front   Don't say that – you've got a lot better.

Back   You said they've been together for years.

Front   Our costume's better. It's traditional – they'll like that.

Back   One of the others told me they have sex in theirs.

Front   How is that even possible?

Back   Linda's sewn in a couple of zips.

Front   Horses don't have zips – it shouldn't be allowed.

Back   What did you think of the ones before us?

Front   Not nearly as good. The pink one was less mobile than Mr. Blobby.

Back   The white one looked all right.

Front   It only had three legs!

Back   Diversity's important in the theatre nowadays.

Front   What about Ben and Pete? They're good dancers, but I'm not sure about the sequins.

Back   Yes, that is unusual on a horse.

Front   What about your mother?

Back   She doesn't wear much with sequins.

Front   The scan. Have they found anything?

Back   She's still waiting for the results.

Front   Is she worried?

Back   She's holding up. Dad's ignoring the whole thing. There's no history of breast cancer in the family, so I think she'll be okay.

Front   Me too.

Back Do you think they've made a decision yet?

Front Geoff and Linda always overrun.

Back I'll go and check.

Back starts to exit but changes his mind.

Back You go.

Front goes and checks, then returns.

Back Do you know how long they're going to be?

Front It should only be a few more minutes. I saw a great place on Winchester Close on the web - viewings start next week.

Back If we get the part, you said they'll start rehearsals next week. How can we do both?

Front We'll just have to fit it all in.

Back Could we postpone it? The house buying.

Front You don't want to move in together, do you?

Back I do...but not just yet.

Front You do love me?

Back Of course I do.

Front Then why wait?

Back I just need to work up to it. I've never lived with someone before – you have. What was it like?

Front Good. Until the rows started. Then it was awful.

Back That won't be us, will it?

Front Not unless you use up all the milk.

Back   I might switch to that almond milk.

Front   What's wrong with normal milk?

Back   It's full of chemicals. Almonds are meant to be good for the complexion. Cleopatra took baths in milk.

Front   You won't be doing that, will you? I couldn't live with someone who kept filling up the bath with semi-skimmed. Look, if you don't want to be with me, just say it.

Back   Of course I do. What if I moved into yours for a couple of weeks?

Front   It will be a bit cramped.

Back   I'll be tidy.

Front   I can empty a drawer for you.

Back   And space in a wardrobe.

Front   Next week?

Back   Next month?

Front   All right then. It's settled. You'll move into mine next month, and this weekend you'll ask for the loan. I wish they'd hurry up.

Front gets up and walks around.

Back   I feel a bit light-headed.

Front   Put your head between your knees.

Back puts his head between his knees.

Front   Is that better?

Back sits back up.

Back   Not really.
Front Shall I get the water?
Back   Let me walk around for a minute.

Back walks about.

Front Better?
Back   Could we put on the rest of the costume?
Front The result should be announced soon.
Back   Why couldn't they just email us?
Front You know Jules – she likes to make a big show of
          this sort of thing.
Back   Does she direct anything other than pantomimes?
Front School plays. And she directed herself in that
          performance piece in the library.
Back   That's right – she had all those feathers stuck in
          her hair. She was some sort of fertility god I think.
Front I don't know how she managed to get so many
          red handkerchiefs stuck up her skirt. When they
          appeared, I saw a little boy burst into tears.
Back   We could do part of the routine?
Front I thought you felt light-headed.
Back   It will help take my mind off things.
Front Let's clear some space. We'll just do the first
          section. Don't forget it's right then left. Do you
          really want to put on the full costume?

Back Actually, let's try it without.

Front We've not got our music.

Back We'll imagine it. Don't go too quickly.

Front and Back dance for less than a minute.

Front You got it right that time.

Back I did. I'm feeling better too.

Front It's always easier when no one's watching.

Back Maybe.

Front I'll go and have another look.

Back No, I'll go.

Back puts on the head and leaves. Back re-enters looking forlorn. But then looks happy, takes off the head.

Back Geoff and Linda were disqualified for 'non-anatomical features'. We got the part.

Front and Back embrace.

Back They didn't say anything about the missed kick. Jules says she's looking forward to having us in the show.

Front I knew you could do it. It looks like we'll be doing this for a few more years.

Back And for next year's show, I'll be at the front.

Lights fade.

A GAME OF TWO HALVES

A Game of Two Halves was produced by Joe Spurgeon at Theatre Royal Bath. It was part of an evening of ten semi-staged rehearsed readings by members of the theatre's Writers' Group under the tuition of playwright/director Matt Grinter. It was staged on 1st September 2019.

CAST ///
BEE: PHOEBE MULCAHY
FROGGIE: TOM MORRIS
REFEREE: ADAM PETERS

DIRECTED BY /// CHLOE MASTERTON

CHARACTERS ///
BEE: WOMAN, 30–40S
FROGGIE: MAN, 30–40S

SETTING ///
THE HOME TERRACE OF A LOWER DIVISION MEN'S FOOTBALL TEAM. BEE AND FROGGIE ARE SEASON TICKET HOLDERS WITH ALLOTTED SEATS. AN ARMCHAIR CAN SYMBOLISE FROGGIE'S PARENTS' HOUSE. THE SCENES OCCUR ON SATURDAY AFTERNOONS, MOVING THROUGH THE SEASON FROM SEPTEMBER TO MAY. A REFEREE (OR OTHER METHODS) INDICATES EACH GAME NUMBER.

AUTHOR'S NOTES ///
/ START SPEAKING NEXT LINE OR INTERRUPTION

GAME 1

*Sunny. Bee sits with an empty seat next to her. Froggie slides
past other seated supporters, exchanging greetings, towards her.
Bee watches him intently. Both wear their team's home shirt.*

Froggie   Hello, Bee.

Bee   Hello, Froggie, it's nice to see you.

Froggie   How was your summer?

Bee   The girls were a handful, but my sister helped
out. Emily's into Barbie and Julie's started
senior school.

Froggie   Won't be long before she's playing truant and
smoking in the park.

Bee   She better bloody not. How was yours?

Froggie   I had to put Mum in the nursing home.

Bee   I'm sorry to hear that.

Froggie   It's all right, it was coming. She'll be with Dad
now, so that's something. It feels like an end of
an era, though. Nine years back at home.

Bee   Must be hard, being in the house alone.

Froggie I get to watch what I want on TV. Eat whenever I like. It's not so bad.

The players come out of the changing rooms onto the pitch.

Froggie Here we go, then, Bee. Ready for another season dreaming of promotion but resigned to mid-table mediocrity?

Bee I never stop dreaming, Froggie.

Froggie Did you attend any of the pre-season matches in Portugal? Some of these likely lads went over.

Bee My ex would never take the girls for that long. I did come to the game here against that makeshift Prem side. I thought you might have been here.

Froggie Nah, I don't like it when there's nothing on the line. Three nil, wasn't it?

Bee We held our own in the second half. The...the...

Bee sneezes and Froggie hands her a handkerchief.

Bee Thank you. It always happens when the kids go back to school. They bring back all sorts.

Froggie One of the advantages of not having any.

Bee *(Blowing nose)* I suppose so.

Players warm up. Froggie reads the programme.

Froggie *(Pronounces the player's name badly)* Looks like that new fella's starting – Manuel Forlan Jimenez.

Bee *(Correctly)* Jimenez.

Froggie Yeah. Where do they get these names, eh?

Bee He's good, nearly scored in the friendly.

Froggie Let's see.

Bee I heard a rumour that we might get new owners: Thai businessmen.

Froggie What?! That's all we bloody need. Foreign owners with no understanding of the history of the club.

Bee Lots of money, though.

Froggie Money's what's wrong with this game. Who do you know that got money that didn't become a prick? That Alfie that ran the greengrocers off the Broadway. Used to be a nice old fella 'til he won the lottery and then *poof*, off he went to the south of France or somewhere. Not heard a peep from him since. It's selfish, that's what it is.

Bee What would you do if you won the lottery?

Froggie I'd invest in the club. Not give it. A sort of interest-free loan. It'd mean they didn't have to sell out to these...these, well, you know.

Bee No. I don't.

Froggie Er, never mind. What would you do?

Bee I've never been to France.

Froggie You should go, take the kids.

Bee   Oh, I don't think I'd be brave enough to go on my own. And I was never very good at languages. Bit pricey too, flights and everything.

Froggie Just bundle everyone in a car.

Bee   That's a good idea. Have you been?

Froggie Just a school trip. Dad thought it was a waste of money. "Who serves hot chocolate in a bowl for breakfast?", he said. "Bloody ridiculous." I still went, though. Mum persuaded him.

Bee   Do you think having money's important?

Froggie Not to me. Family's number one, always. When Dad took me here the first time, he made me look at all these people around us. "This club will never let you down, son. Not like people. It doesn't matter whether they win, lose or draw, they'll always be here for you." Who told you about the takeover?

Bee   Walter.

Froggie Walter? Top gent. Longest serving chairman of the Supporters' Club.

Froggie looks behind and up to the corporate boxes.

Froggie There he is, underneath the corporate boxes.

Froggie waves at Walter.

Froggie I'll catch him after the game. See if we can get something going.

Bee   What do you mean?

Froggie   A petition. Placards. The works. Show them that the club belongs to the fans.

Bee   It might affect the team.

Froggie   What does it matter if we drop a few extra places? Finish twelfth instead of tenth? At least we'll be the same.

Bee   Maybe someone new would be a good / thing.

Froggie jumps up.

Froggie   No one can stop us if we stick together! We'll do whatever it takes. Not go to away games, turn our backs on the pitch. We'll fight them all the way!

Bee   The game's starting, sit down.

Froggie sits down. Whistle blows for kick-off.

GAME 10

Overcast. It's near the end of the second half. Bee and Froggie are standing. Froggie gesticulates at the linesman.

Froggie   You need to get your eyes tested.

Bee   Got any plans for tomorrow night?

Froggie   Not really. (To linesman) That was offside, you muppet. I ought to come down there and stick that flag up your /

Bee   I'm taking the girls to Victoria Park for the fireworks.

Froggie   Oh, right.

Froggie claps a tackle made by Peters.

Froggie   Good job, Peters.

Bee   It's near you, isn't it?

Froggie   What?

Bee   Victoria Park.

Froggie   Round the corner. Bloody fireworks. Can't stand the things. Money shot straight into the air while the parents try to stop their little brats poking each other in the eye with sparklers.

Bee   I'll take that as a no, then.

Jimenez is one on one with the opposition keeper.

Froggie   Hold on, here we go...Oh for Chrissakes, Jimmy, I
           could have scored that with my eyes closed.
Bee   Jimmy? Oh, Jimenez.
Froggie   Six games, no goals. Waste of flipping money.
Bee   Give him a chance.
Froggie   Why? He gets paid a fortune to score goals, not
           just run around looking pretty. Might as well put
           you out there.

Added time board shown.

Bee   One minute to go. He was top scorer in Segunda B
           two years running.
Froggie   It's one thing to be swanning about in the
           sunshine in Italy /
Bee   Spain.
Froggie   Whatever. But this is England. He's got to get
           stuck in, put his head where he might / lose it.

Bee points at Jimenez on the pitch.

Bee   Look!

Crowd grows animated.

Froggie   Go on, son, that's it, keep / going!
Bee   Come on, come / on!
Froggie   Shoot!

Crowd erupts as Jimenez scores.

Froggie Jimmy, you beauty!

Bee and Froggie celebrate.

Bee I told you.
Bee and Froggie Jim–my! Jim–my! Jim–my!

Whistle blows.

Froggie Great win.
Bee If you change your mind / about Sunday.

Froggie gets up.

Froggie I've got to go, Bee. Meeting in the Lion. Planning
our campaign of resistance. See you next week.

Froggie exits.

Bee Bye.

GAME 16

Overcast. It's half-time. Bee sits and Froggie approaches with a half-eaten pie and two teas, handing one to Bee.

Froggie   Here you go.
Bee   Cheers.
Froggie   *(Offering the pie)* Want a bite?
Bee   No, thanks.
Froggie   Right, here we go.

Froggie stands and turns back to the pitch.

Froggie   Come on, then.

Bee stands up and turns around.

Froggie   I heard they're here.
Bee   Who?
Froggie   The Asians.
Bee   The Chanakathibets. Where?
Froggie   *(Indicating)* Up there.
Bee   Too late, then.
Froggie   Never too late, Bee. We'll fight them to the end.
                 Even if we lose, they'll know how we feel.
Bee   I heard it's already happened, Froggie.

Bee turns around and sits down. Froggie follows.

Froggie   What do you mean?

Bee   My sister's best mates with Marion. The club's bookkeeper. She told her it's a done deal.

Froggie   That's it, then.

Bee   Might not be so bad.

Froggie   Might not be so bad? This is the end. This is...I can't believe it. Mr Chana...Chanakath...

Bee   Chanakathibet.

Froggie   Him. He promised to listen to us, hear our demands, respect our wishes. And now they've stabbed us in the back.

Bee   They said they're going to make lots of improvements. A women's team, free youth training for kids on Saturdays. Veggie pies.

Froggie   My God. I'd never have believed it, our club selling out like this. To someone like them.

Froggie stands, turns and hurls the pie towards the corporate boxes.

Bee   Don't!

Froggie   Traitors!

Off-stage stewards observe what he's done and ask him to leave his seat.

Froggie   Okay, okay, I'm coming.

Froggie hands Bee his tea and exits.

GAME 19

Snowing. Bee sits alone. At home in a chintz armchair Froggie wears a pair of headphones to listen to the games.

GAME 24

Wintry. They celebrate a goal.

GAME 29

Cold. Bee sits holding the handkerchief. Froggie holds a phrase book.

Froggie Je voudrais acheter un billet pour le match.

GAME 34

Spring sunshine. Bee jumps up.

Bee   The referee's a wank /
Froggie À quelle heure commence le match de football?

GAME 39

Spring sunshine. Bee sits eating a pie. Froggie pushes seat off stage.

GAME 43

Sunny. Bee sits. Froggie arrives and sits down.
Bee ignores Froggie.

Froggie (*Correct pronunciation*) Jimenez turned out good after all, might make the play-offs. Best goal difference in the division. Build on a solid defence and one day we might get promoted. Always said, didn't I?

Bee You were only banned for ten games.

Froggie I know, I'm...I've never missed a game, you know that. Getting banned by the club I loved all my life. Made me think. I wasn't going to come back at all. They don't deserve my support, standing here, in all weathers, while these...these players get paid a fortune to run about, free to go wherever they want.

Bee So, why'd you come back?

Froggie Because of...well, you never know who you're going to be sitting next to. I thought, I can't do that to Bee, not fair on her to have someone she hardly knows turning up each week. Besides, I didn't want to give them the satisfaction of knowing they'd won. It's still my club, whoever owns it.

[Stage direction:] *Bee hands him back his handkerchief, clean and neatly folded.*

GAME 44

Sunny. They've swapped seats. Both feel uncomfortable and change back.

THE PLAY-OFF SEMI-FINAL

Sunny. They are standing. Froggie's hands are over his eyes.

Froggie   Who's taking it?
Bee   Peters.

Froggie removes his hands from his eyes.

Froggie   Peters?! (*Pronounced correctly*) What about Jimenez?
Bee   Peter's the dedicated taker.
Froggie   I know that, but Jimmy's sur le feu. We win this, we're in the final. This is no effing time for sticking to the rules. I can't watch.

Froggie covers his face.

Bee   Hold on, was that French?

Peters scores and the crowd goes wild. Bee and Froggie celebrate.

THE PLAY-OFF FINAL

Sunny. They both sit. Bee is wearing the club's new strip, partly obscured by her coat. Youth team players are running drills.

Froggie Is it true?

Bee They've sold Jimenez; going back to Spain.

Froggie A pity. Could have built a great team around the lad. Must be the weather; can't take our winters.

Bee At the Supporters' Club meeting, someone said he'd slept with the manager's wife.

Froggie Jesus. Supporters' Club, eh?

Bee Treasurer. Said my bookkeeping qualifications made me the best candidate.

Froggie Fair play to them. I'm not wearing the new strip, though.

Bee zips up her coat.

Froggie Disgraceful, changing the colour. It's sacrilege.

Bee Are you going to renew your season ticket?

Froggie I don't know, to be honest. Been a lot of changes this year. If we win this and go up, season ticket prices gonna rocket. Lots to think about.

Bee I'm coming back, whatever happens.

Froggie I see, well, I probably will. Good seats these. You know, I've never been so nervous. I might get the teas now.

Bee Wait to half-time, it's good to keep some things the same.

Froggie How's Julie settled in at her new school?

Bee She had a few wobbles at the start, but she's loving it now. They play football.

Froggie She any good?

Bee Made our youth team. (*Pointing at the pitch*) Look, there she is.

They watch Julie train.

Bee She's seen us. Wave.

Bee waves. Julie waves back. Froggie holds up his hand.

Froggie I thought she saw her dad on Saturdays?

Bee One in two now, because of this.

Froggie She been to a game yet?

Bee Never.

Froggie You know, they're doing a special on family season tickets for next year. Keeping the prices the same. You don't need to be a real family or anything, just two adults and at least one kid. Works out cheaper than two adult season tickets.

Bee Maybe we should do that?

Froggie We'd have to move over there, lose these seats, but still, could be worth a go.

Bee Never hurts to try something new.

The whistle blows for kick-off. Lights out.

CHAINSAW

Chainsaw was performed as part of an evening of six short plays in aid of Time To Talk Day on 6th February 2020. It was organised by Scott Davenport and all proceeds went to the Time to Change charity. The venue was The King's Arms Theatre in Salford and the play was directed by Michelle Parker.

CAST ///
ANNA: KAREN SHARPLES
INDIA: ABIGAIL BOSTON

CHARACTERS ///
ANNA: LATE-30S TO MID-40S WOMAN
INDIA: EARLY TO MID-20S WOMAN

SETTING ///
WE ARE IN BLACKNESS

AUTHOR'S NOTES ///
/ BEGIN SPEAKING NEXT LINE

SCENE 1

A phone vibrates and flashes on a hard surface. It repeats. Silence. A doorbell rings. It rings again, more insistently. A light comes on, revealing the phone on the table in a lounge-hallway leading to the front door. A sleepy woman, Anna, in night clothes, enters the lounge-hallway. The doorbell rings again.

Anna   Okay, okay, I'm coming.

Anna checks the phone, then opens the door. A younger, flustered woman, India, who's been looking through the letterbox, stumbles inside, holding a computer tablet.

Anna   (*Sarcastically*) Please, come in.
India   Sorry, I...
Anna   Better have a really good explanation for waking me up at midnight.
India   It's not, is it? It can't be. (*Checks tablet*) We've still got time. Look, this may come as a shock but /
Anna   You could say that.
India   Please, it's an emergency, I need / you
Anna   I don't see no flashing lights.

India   I did call.

Anna   Who are you and how did you get my number?

India   That doesn't matter. Well, it does, but not right now. We need to get hold of your son.

Anna   My son?

India   We think he's in danger. So if you could call him, to check he's / okay.

Anna   Why don't you call him, since you seem to be so good at getting people's numbers?

India   I couldn't find his. Look, this is really urgent, you need to check if he's safe.

Anna   What are you talking about? Has something happened to him?

India   Not yet, but it might do, very soon. Please, could you just ring him to be sure?

Anna picks up her phone and begins to dial.

Anna   He'll be asleep?

India   He's not.

Anna cancels the call.

Anna   What the hell are you talking about? How do you know that? Do you know him? He said he'd been seeing someone new but...

India   Please call him.

Anna   Not until you tell me what the hell's going on?

India   I'm a volunteer for a group that tries to intervene in suicides.

Anna   And you think my son...Don't be ridiculous.

India   Please, just call him to make sure. (*Checks tablet*) We've only got a few minutes.

Anna   What are you talking about?

India   He said he was going to kill himself at midnight.

Anna   You're off your head. I only spoke to him yesterday, he was fine. He was having some issues with this girlfriend, but that's normal at his age, isn't it?

India   Would you just call him? Our system says it's an eighty-three per cent probability.

Anna   What do you mean, system?

India   It's an AI...artificial intelligence...that scans message boards and social postings for key words and phrases that suggest someone might be about to self-harm.

Anna   Is that legal?

India   Does that matter right now?

Anna   Well, yes, if you're going to expect me to ring up my perfectly happy son just on some computer's say-so. Plus, if it's anything like the ones at work, it's probably wrong.

India   We've saved over a dozen people this year.

Anna   Saved?

India   Yes, saved.

Anna   How do you know they want to be?

India   Of course they do.

Anna	Were you there for each one?
India	No.
Anna	So how do you know for sure?
India	I...Well, why wouldn't they? After we've helped them, they get help and come to realise it was just a moment where things got out of hand, became too much.
Anna	That's rather presumptuous. And who makes you the best judge?
India	I'm studying for a PhD in psychology.
Anna	You're just a student. Are you being paid to do this?
India	No. I'm a volunteer, but we've had training.
Anna	Really? So you'd know what to do if you turned up at someone's door and there's some crazy person brandishing a chainsaw? You can handle that?
India	That's not going to happen, and if it did, we'd call the police. And we don't say crazy, it's neurodiverse.
Anna	Is it?
India	Some of us believe that there is no singular type of normal human behaviour, but a whole range, including those that have been called mad, mentally ill or crazy. In fact, it may be society's inability to accommodate some of these people that's driving them to self-harm.
Anna	And how did you say you found them?
India	The AI has a database of words and phrases that are linked to an increased likelihood to self-harm. When

the system finds a probability over seventy-five per cent, it notifies the nearest person. In this case, me. (*Checks tablet*) Please, it will be midnight soon.

Anna My son would never do anything like that. Kill himself. No, you must have got the wrong person. There's no way my son wouldn't tell me if something serious was wrong.

India He told you that he was having some issues with his new girlfriend.

Anna Yes, but he was perfectly fine.

India checks her tablet.

India He split up with her weeks ago. He just found out that she's dating his best friend and believes they were seeing each other behind his back.

Anna (*Making a grab for the tablet but failing*) Let me see.

India No.

Anna Well, he's just saying that because he wants some attention. He used to do that all the time. He doesn't really mean it.

India Are you sure?

Anna My son's tough, like me. He'd tell me if he was feeling that bad.

India Most parents are unaware of their children's true state of mind. Particularly young men. If you just called him, you could be sure. It would give you peace of mind, wouldn't it?

Anna   Why didn't you call him, instead of coming here?

India   I couldn't find his number, but I found yours. When there's so little time, we have to go with whatever method's the quickest.

Anna   You're too young to have children.

India   I don't see why that's / relevant.

Anna   If you did, you might have some idea what it's like to get to know someone so well you can tell what they're thinking at any moment. I used to know what he'd ask for for tea, before he'd even said anything. If you asked me now, I could still tell you what the first thing would be he'd eat on the plate.

India   Please! There isn't the time for this.

India tries to grab Anna's phone and they tussle.

Anna   Get the hell off me! (*Retains phone*) Do you think some computer knows my son better than his own mother?

India   Many parents are never aware of their children's deteriorating mental health. Leaving home, girlfriends, coursework can all bring existing or new mental health disorders to the surface.

Anna   My son's never had anything wrong with him. Why are YOU doing this?

India   Does it matter?

Anna   If you want me to ring him, yes, it does.

India   Because my best friend killed herself last year.

Anna   I'm sorry. You don't have to / say any more.

India   I want to. She'd been diagnosed as bipolar, but she always said it didn't matter. I think I was more upset than her. She said it was her SUPERPOWER and I was a mere mortal who she'd have to protect from now on. And she did. We were at a club; I'd had my drink spiked by this bloke who took me and put me into his car. She found me and pulled me out. All I can remember is her screaming. He knocked out two of her teeth. The bouncers said she wouldn't let go of me until the ambulance arrived. I don't know what would have happened if she hadn't come outside. But when she needed me, I wasn't there... (*She cries*)

Anna goes to comfort her, but India rejects her. Anna phones her son.

Anna   Hello...Yes, it's your mum. I know...it's nearly midnight. I just wanted to check you're okay...Yes, I know I could have done that during the day but... You would tell me if anything was wrong, wouldn't you? If something was bothering you...Yes, I know, I thought so...Well, goodnight, love.

Anna ends the call.

Anna   Well, there you go, then.
India   Thank you. It's good to hear he's okay.
Anna   Would you like a drink?

India   No, I'll just go. I've got to see my supervisor in the morning.

Anna shows India to the door.

Anna   I'm sorry about your friend. I don't believe you could have stopped it, however much you might have tried.

India   Maybe.

Anna opens the door.

Anna   Well, best of luck with (*indicating tablet*) this. Your heart's in the right place.

India   Thank you and I'm sorry if I scared you.

Anna   You didn't.

India   Well, then I'm sorry that we woke up Henry unnecessarily.

Anna   Henry?

India   Your son. (*Checks tablet*) Henry...Stanton.

Anna   My surname's Stanton. It's our mother's surname, she was a bit of a feminist, so she insisted we both keep it. But I don't have a son called Henry...he's called Oliver...but...

India   What?

Anna   My sister's son's called Henry. What time is it?

End.

HIT POINTS

Hit Points was written in 2019.

CHARACTERS ///
SAMANTHA: 42
JOE: 15
HALEY: 39
BARRY: 45

SETTING ///
A KITCHEN–LIVING ROOM AT THE BACK OF A POST-WAR
TERRACED HOUSE. ON ONE SIDE IS THE KITCHEN AREA WITH
AN ISLAND. IN THE CENTRE, A GLASS-PANELLED DOOR LEADS
TO THE REST OF THE HOUSE. ON THE OTHER SIDE, A SOFA
FACES A TELEVISION. A GAMES CONSOLE SITS BETWEEN
THEM ON A COFFEE TABLE. COLOURFUL PAINTINGS ADORN
THE WALLS.

AUTHOR'S NOTES ///
/ INDICATES THAT THE NEXT CHARACTER SHOULD START
SPEAKING OR BEGIN ACTION

SCENE 1

Joe lies on his back on the sofa, a baseball cap covering his face. Samantha enters and lifts her handbag onto the breakfast table, registering a twinge. Joe mumbles.

Samantha Joe?

Samantha peers over the sofa.

Samantha Are you awake, love?

Joe turns over. Samantha removes his cap then turns off the television. She swings the handbag onto her shoulder and leaves quietly.

SCENE 2

Samantha unpacks food shopping on the island as Joe, wearing a headset, plays a cooperative combat game.

Joe   (*To teammates*) I'm taking the left flank.

Samantha takes out a folded letter from a drawer in the breakfast bar and reads it.

Samantha Joe, I need to talk to you about something.

Joe What time's tea?

Samantha It's veggie burgers, so not long. Chips or waffles?

Joe Either. No, waffles. (*To teammates*) There's someone on that ridge.

Samantha Joe, could you log out?

Joe (*To teammate*) Great shot, Mehmet...The bazooka was a bit overkill...Yeah, I know you took out the tank too...*Hilarious.*

Samantha rips off his headset.

Joe Hey!

Samantha I need to speak to you.

Joe I'm in the middle of a game. They need me.

Samantha They'll have to manage without you.

Joe Can I at least tell them? (*Looking at the screen*) Dead.

Samantha hands back the headset. Joe puts it on.

Joe Sorry, guys...Yeah, yeah, I know, sitting duck... You'll have to stay alive without me...You *know* that's the truth...I need to go...I've not forgotten about the tournament...I'll log in / later.

Samantha turns the console off.

Joe Mum!

Samantha I don't care, this is important. Can you help me put those tins in the cupboard?

They return to the kitchen. Samantha hands tins to Joe, who puts them away.

Joe Is there anything to eat?
Samantha There's fruit in the bowl.

Joe dismisses the offer. Samantha hands him a snack, which he eats as they continue to unpack.

Samantha I swear you're eating more than any human can possibly burn off. Do you remember I told you I'd been feeling a bit run-down?

Joe shrugs.

Samantha Well, I went to the doctor and they took some blood. They'll be doing some more tests and it's nothing to worry about, but you should be prepared, just in case.
Joe Is it serious?
Samantha Probably not, but / if it is...
Joe That's okay, then. Can I go back / to the game?
Samantha But if it is something...we'll need to think about who can help look after you.
Joe I can look after myself.

Samantha Well, not legally, you can't. And I remember the kitchen after you'd had your footie friends over.

Joe That was just the once.

Samantha What about your bedroom?

Joe Okay, okay.

Samantha What I'm saying is that you might need to spend more time with other people. Like your father.

Joe (*Enthusiastic*) Really?!

Samantha You'd like that?

Joe Dad lets me play when I want.

Samantha I've told him about that. Anyway, I've not spoken to him yet and it probably won't be necessary. You could stay over at your dad's one night?

Joe Sounds good.

Samantha But if anything happened while you were with him, you'd tell me, wouldn't you?

Joe Can I go back online now?

Samantha Joe, this is serious.

Joe Alright, I will.

Samantha You know I love you, don't you?

Joe Yes.

Samantha You *can* say it back.

Joe (*Inaudible*) I love you.

Samantha I didn't hear that.

Joe I love you.

Samantha Thank you.

Joe Can I go back online now?

Samantha Why don't you ever meet your friends from the game? You could invite *them* round.

Joe laughs.

Samantha What?

Joe Mehmet, that's SuperSniper89, lives in Istanbul. JensTheTiger is in some town in Denmark we can't pronounce without killing ourselves, and Zoe lives in Brussels. So unless you've won the lottery, we won't be hanging out.

Samantha You're in a mood today. Do you even know what they look like? Or how old they are?

Joe Why does that matter?

Samantha You don't know who to trust online. That's why I prefer you playing here, rather than in your room. So you don't know anything about them?

Joe Jens designs websites from home. He's got three goldfish: Harry, Larry and Mo. Something to do with a film, I think. Mehmet's at college, he's twenty-two and studying maths. He plans to marry when he graduates. Zoe, she's at school like me and does these really cool charcoal drawings. Can I go back online now?

Samantha One hour.

Joe goes back online.

Joe Actually, could I have chips? (*To teammates*) Hey, guys I'm back...but I've not got long so let's make it count.

SCENE 3

Alone, Joe's playing online.

Joe   Hey, everyone...What do you mean, late?...
Okay, five minutes, I'll give you that...Hold on,
I'm not even last...Where's Jens?...No, I don't
know where he is...His number?...Like a phone
number?...No, I don't...wait, I might do...He
offered to help me with some homework...I'll
look for it later...He's probably just been
grounded...Let's go.

SCENE 4

*Samantha's helping Joe put on his coat as he gets ready to leave
for an overnight with his father, Barry. A car horn sounds.*

Samantha Are you sure you've got everything?
Joe   Yes.
Samantha You've got your football kit for tomorrow?

Joe lifts his sports bag.

Joe   I'm not a kid.
Samantha I know, but you've never stayed overnight
somewhere without me.
Joe   Dad's waiting.

Samantha You've got your new pyjamas?

Joe I don't wear pyjamas any more.

Samantha I only just bought that pair. Give me a hug before you go.

Joe lets Samantha hug him. Joe leaves. Samantha spots Joe's phone on the breakfast bar and picks it up. She waits, holding his phone. Joe returns, takes his phone and leaves. Samantha makes a call.

Samantha Yes, he's gone...Half an hour's fine...What shall I order?...Okay, I'll wait till you get here...Bye.

SCENE 5

Samantha and Haley drink wine. Fast food containers litter the breakfast bar.

Samantha Please don't make me.

Haley You'll look amazing. You've got the legs for it.

Samantha Posh?!

Haley Tanya wasn't too keen on being Sporty until I reminded her about that duet she did with Bryan.

Samantha Do you think they...

Haley No, he was married.

Samantha I know, but still.

Haley Isn't it about time you got back on the old horse?

Samantha Not yet.
Haley You should go online.
Samantha I couldn't.

Samantha takes Haley's empty glass. Haley points her phone at Samantha.

Samantha What are you doing?

Haley takes a picture.

Samantha Hey!

Samantha struggles to open a new bottle of wine. Haley enters text on her phone.

Haley Right, you're up.
Samantha What do you mean, *up*?
Haley You're now online dating. Swipe right for Bryan and left for Gibson.
Samantha Let me see.

Samantha looks at Haley's phone.

Samantha I'll delete it later.
Haley Sam, you've got to get out there. You were just unlucky.
Samantha I had more than a photo to go on. We'd known

each other all through college. How did I not see what he was really like?

Haley Don't blame yourself.

Samantha What if he loses his temper with Joe while I'm not there?

Haley Has he ever done something like that before?

Samantha Not really.

Haley Go on.

Samantha It wasn't his fault, I / was partly

Haley Sam!

Samantha Well, it wasn't, not really. I said I'd take Joe to the county trials, but I'd been so rattled with Barry's job and issues at the clinic, I'd completely forgotten about it. And you know how Joe is with remembering things, so anyway, he missed the trials. It wasn't really that important to him, but Barry was furious. I thought Joe was upstairs, but he must have come down while we were arguing. Barry grabbed my arm. Now, it didn't hurt, it looked worse than it was, but Joe must have seen it through the glass. He came storming in just as I shook myself loose. Well, Barry's arm went back and caught Joe across the face.

Haley That's awful.

Samantha It just glanced him. I'm not sure who was more shocked, Joe or Barry. After that, Barry calmed down a lot, but I'd had enough. You know the rest.

Haley And you trust him with Joe?

Samantha It doesn't matter if I do or don't, the court's given him a day a week.

Haley But not overnight.

Samantha Well, it might be more than that if I can't find anyone else.

Samantha gets up and goes to the kitchen.

Haley What are you talking about?

Samantha takes out the note and returns with it.

Haley What's going on?

She hands it to Haley, who reads it.

Haley Oh God.

SCENE 6

Samantha's on the phone.

Samantha Mother, I know you want to help...Please stop crying...I know, I know...But Joe's not like that any more...Why don't you put Dad on...No, I know it's your choice too, but I want to hear what he has to say.

Joe comes in.

Samantha Hi, love.

Joe assesses the fruit bowl. Samantha hands him an apple and he slumps on the sofa to eat it.

Samantha Oh, hi, Dad...Yeah, yeah, I know. I'm okay, really. Just tired sometimes...Joe's fine. How are the leeks?...Stolen?! That's terrible.

Samantha and Joe stifle laughs.

Samantha Do you have a suspect?

Joe jumps on the sofa, pretending to be a rabbit.

Samantha You think it's one of the other allotment holders?...Surely not...Who?...*He's always been an admirer of your leeks*...

Samantha and Joe laugh.

Samantha Well, I hope you catch them.

Joe sits back down on the sofa.

Samantha I know...I wouldn't ask otherwise...No, there's not really anyone else...Yes, I know, you're very busy and...but...and that's how you both feel,

is it?...Fine. (*Tearful*) Yes, I know it's not about
him...Uh-huh, yes, I'll let you know if anything
changes...Yes, I'll tell him...Goodbye. (*Pause*) Joe.

Joe   Yeah.

Samantha Gran and Grandad say hi.

SCENE 7

*Joe is on the phone to Jens. He picks up Samantha's new cane
and plays with it.*

Joe   I thought maybe you'd been banned from
playing, my mum does that...She's ill too...I
can't remember, *somethingosis*...I hope you get
better...Oh, I see...The tournament's next week,
what shall I tell the others?...If you're sure...No,
okay, I won't say anything...Bye.

SCENE 8

*Samantha's unpacking Joe's sports bag as Joe examines a
new headset.*

Samantha (*Smelling the bag*) Oh, boy! Could your dad not
have washed your kit?

Joe   He was busy.

Samantha Busy looking after you. Did you win the match?

Joe   I think so.

Samantha	How could you not know?
Joe	It's just a football match.
Samantha	Whatever. Did you enjoy spending more time with him?
Joe	Yeah.
Samantha	I missed having you here. What's he given you?
Joe	New headset. Top-of-the-range one.
Samantha	How'd he afford that?
Joe	He got promoted.
Samantha	Did he?
Joe	And a bonus.
Samantha	Anything else?
Joe	Not really.

Joe gets ready to go online.

Samantha	*Joe.*
Joe	(*Mumbling*) A new girlfriend.
Samantha	What?! How long's that been going on for?
Joe	A while.
Samantha	Why didn't you say anything? Never mind. What's she like?
Joe	Nice.
Samantha	Not much to go on. Does she stay overnight?
Joe	I think so.
Samantha	Looks like your dad's turning things around.
Joe	How long before dinner?
Samantha	If you helped, it could be a lot quicker.

Joe   But I want to try this.

Samantha Half an hour, then you can peel some potatoes.

Joe goes online.

SCENE 9

Samantha's getting ready to go out. Joe hovers nearby.

Samantha I've left you instructions for dinner. If you can't
             wait, make yourself a snack. I shouldn't be too
             long, the woman who runs the support group
             said it usually finishes on time. I should be back
             about eight. You going to be okay?

Joe   Yeah.

Samantha Well, that's reassuring.

She kisses him.

Samantha Bye, love.

*Samantha leaves. Joe takes two slices of bread and puts them
into the toaster. He adjusts the settings and lowers the bread.
He sits on the sofa, puts on his headset and logs in. He plays
online, talking occasionally.*

*As he plays, the toast starts to burn. The smoke alarm sounds
and, hearing it, he rushes to the kitchen. He pops the toaster and*

waves the smoke about with a tea towel. The alarm stops.
Joe finds that the toast is stuck inside. He takes out a fork and
starts stabbing inside the toaster. There's a spark and the lights
go out.

SCENE 10

Joe's playing online.

Joe   I know, I know, I didn't see them...Well,
             Jens is usually in that position...I know he's
             better...I did...He's fine, he just can't play at the
             moment...I think he said he was doing exams...
             No, I don't know which ones...He said he'd try
             to come back...He didn't say when...I know the
             tournament's soon...Replace him? We can't.

Samantha enters using her cane, carrying shopping.

Joe   Okay, okay, I'll call him back. (*Joe sees*
             Samantha) Look, I've got to go. Ciao, losers.

Joe exits the game.

SCENE 11

Samantha and Joe are sitting on the sofa together,
watching television.

Samantha Do you need to practise?

Joe Not yet.

Samantha Joe, I'll be going on some new medication tomorrow. It might slow or even halt the progression.

Joe That's great.

Samantha But there's some side effects and if they get too much, I might have to stop taking them.

Joe But then you won't get better.

Samantha It's not that simple. Look, don't worry about it for now, but we're going to have to think more seriously about who's going to look after you. I spoke to Grandad again, he said you could help him on the allotment.

Joe Digging? No, thanks.

Samantha We're running out of options, love. Barry's parents live too far away. What about Haley?

Joe She's fun.

Samantha Well, that's certainly true. I've not talked to her about it yet, but if you're sure, I'll ask her?

Joe What about Dad?

Samantha Let's see how the overnights go first. Don't worry, love, we'll find a solution.

Joe   What if we don't?

Samantha Let's not think about that now.

Joe   I'd have to go into a foster home, wouldn't I?

Samantha Don't be silly, it won't come to that. It's more likely you'd have to live with your father. But I'll do everything to keep things the same. You've got your GCSEs next year, after all.

Joe   You promise?

Samantha I do. Pinky promise.

They touch their little fingers together.

Joe   I should go / online.

Samantha Okay.

Samantha moves to the kitchen. Joe logs on.

Joe   Hey, guys...Yes, I know I'm late...Who's StealthBomberX2?...And PowerTilly?...No one said anything about new teammates...I did ask him to come back...Oh, so you know about his illness?...He told me not to tell you...I know we're a team, but...I didn't betray anyone...One week?...I'll miss the tournament...That's not fair, I was the second one on this team, you can't...Unanimous?...I see...Well, fuck you!

Samantha Joe!

Joe throws off his headphones and leaves.

Samantha What's wrong?

Joe slams the door.

SCENE 12

Joe is moping about; Samantha sits on the sofa.

Samantha Why don't you show me how to play?
Joe   What?! No, you won't like it.
Samantha Because I'm too old?
Joe   No, it's just...
Samantha What, then?
Joe   It doesn't matter.

Joe sets up the system and helps his mother put on some headphones. They log in and play.

Joe   (*Pointing at the screen*) That's you:
                ShadowWarrior99.
Samantha With the pink hair?!
Joe   We can change it if you don't like it.
Samantha No, leave it.

Joe shows Samantha how to control her character.

Joe   Right, so, this one's to move and these are to fire: this for the machine gun and that one for grenades.

Samantha So where are the baddies?

Joe   They're not baddies, they're other people working in teams, usually four, so we won't stand much of a chance.

Samantha (*Pointing at the screen*) What's that?

Joe   It's just a message. You can send messages to other players you know. Ignore it.

Samantha But they're using your real name.

Joe   It's no one. The game's starting, get ready. Just follow me. If you see your character turn red, that means you've been shot, so move or hide. Look for the yellow flashing icons, then fire.

The game starts. Joe's expertise keeps them alive.

Joe   Stay close.

Samantha I think I got one.

Joe   That was me.

They continue.

Samantha I'm dead.

Joe continues until his character is killed. They take off the headsets.

Samantha How'd we do?

Joe Seventh. Not bad.

Samantha That person's messaged you again. Zoe. She's asking who I am? Why don't you / reply?

Joe turns off the system and leaves.

Samantha Joe. Joe, honey, what's the matter?

Joe slams the door.

SCENE 13

Samantha's tidying up the lounge area. Barry enters unseen and watches her.

Samantha (*Seeing him*) God, you frightened me! I thought you were going to give the keys back.

Barry You said you'd changed your mind because of...

Samantha Well...at least ring the doorbell first. What do you want?

Barry You said you wanted to speak to me.

Samantha You could have just called me back.

Barry I had a job nearby.

Samantha I hear things are going well.

Barry They are. Drinking less too and I've got / a

Samantha New girlfriend.

Barry   Joe told you. You know he and I are getting on
            better than ever.

Samantha That's what I wanted to talk to you about. The
            new medication doesn't seem to be working, so
            we'll need to think about how we look after Joe.

Barry approaches.

Barry   Is there nothing else they can do?

Samantha They're running out of options.

Barry holds her.

Barry   I'm sorry. You look so well; I can't believe it.
            Do you remember you wanted to change the
            wedding vows? Too pessimistic, you said.

Samantha Well, we didn't, did we? Anyway, it doesn't
            matter now.

Barry   It could, if you wanted it to. I didn't want
            to leave, you know that. I've changed, I
            really have.

Samantha Have you?

*Barry leans in, preparing to kiss Samantha. She hesitates before
pulling away.*

Samantha But I've not.

Barry   Sam, come on.

Samantha You've got a girlfriend.

Barry That's not it though, is it? What would make things go back to the way they were?

Samantha That's not what I want to talk about right now. I need to know Joe'll be okay if I ask my lawyer to request that you can have more time with him.

Barry The overnight went well. Really well.

Samantha Joe said *Tina* was there.

Barry There's nothing in the agreement that says she can't be.

Samantha I know and I am happy about it. What if Joe stayed over for longer, perhaps a couple of days at / a time?

Barry That'd be great.

Samantha And he'd be safe?

Barry Safe!? You mean, will I hit him? Jesus, Sam, you know I'd never do that.

Samantha Do I? Don't you / remember?

Barry Hang on, that was an accident. I didn't know he was standing there; you know that.

Samantha I didn't tell my lawyer.

Barry And I'm grateful. But what do you actually think?

Samantha Does it matter?

Barry It does to me. I need to know I can rely on you. Tell me what you think!

Samantha It was an accident, okay.

Barry When will you write to your lawyer?

Samantha It's not definite, there might be other options.

Barry Like what?

Samantha My parents. Haley.

Barry Haley! You've got to be joking. She can't stay in a job for more than two seconds. Her love life's a mess and / she

Samantha Don't talk about her like that, she's my best friend. She'll help if I ask her.

Barry She made a pass at me once.

Samantha What?!

Barry She was in one of those fancy bars on the Harbourside. She could hardly stand. Came over / and

Samantha You're lying.

Barry Pushed herself up against me and made me buy her a drink. You can't trust her.

Samantha I don't believe you.

Barry Ask her.

Samantha I...I've had enough of this, get out.

Barry I dare you.

Samantha Get out!

Barry moves to the door.

Barry You need me, Sam.

SCENE 14

Samantha's alone, playing online, when she receives a call request, which she accepts.

Samantha Hello. Can you hear me?...Is that Zoe?...His new
gaming partner?...No, I'm his mother...Joe?
He's fine, thanks...No, I didn't know he'd left
the team. I mean, I knew he didn't seem to be
playing much but...Seventh sounds good...Much
worse than last year, I didn't know that...Yes,
I'll tell him. Goodbye.

SCENE 15

Samantha drinks at the breakfast bar as Haley hangs up her coat.

Haley She's incredible. Just repeats everything that's
been said the day before as if it's her idea. And
no one says anything. No one. Do you remember
I told you I applied for that job in London? Well,
I've got an interview.

Samantha Really?! But you wouldn't take it, you always
said you hated London.

Haley Depends on what the offer is. It'd be a great job,
but moving, it's a bit scary.

Samantha It would be.

Haley How are you?

Samantha I'm doing okay. I've reduced my hours at the clinic. Some afternoons I could barely keep my eyes open.

Haley Will you be okay for money?

Samantha My parents said they'd help with that.

Haley (*Indicating Samantha's wine glass*) Got one for me?

Samantha Oh, sorry, yes.

Samantha finds a glass and pours.

Haley How's Joe?

Samantha He's doing okay, considering.

Haley How much have you told him?

Samantha Most of it.

Haley Are you sure that's wise?

Samantha *Yes.*

Haley Okay, okay.

Samantha Sorry. I'm just a bit wound up at the moment. I'm trying to do what's best for Joe, but I'm running out of options. My parents don't want their idyllic retirement upset by a 'surly' teenager, so that pretty much just leaves Barry.

Haley Beggar's choice.

Samantha He's keen to see more of Joe, as is Joe for that matter. I just don't know if I can trust him.

Haley I can help out more, you know Joe and I always have a good time together.

Samantha   Would you? That'd be great. It might not come to it, but it's just reassuring to know you'll be here for us...him.

Haley   What sort of things would you need help with?

Samantha   Picking him up from football practice or being here when he gets home, if I'm at the support group.

Haley   That's no problem.

Samantha   Thanks, Haley, that means so much.

Samantha kisses Haley.

Haley   Anything to stop you having to trust him with Barry.

Samantha   I'll call my lawyer tomorrow. There's no guarantee the court will agree. Barry's bound to object, but it should go through. I *can* rely on you, can't I?

Haley   Of course.

Samantha   I mean, you've not done anything I should know about?

Haley   What are you talking about? This is silly, you know there's no secrets between us.

Samantha   I know, I know. It's just something someone said?

Haley   Who, Joe?

Samantha   No, not Joe. Barry.

Haley   Barry?!

Samantha   Yes.

Haley   What's he got to do with me?

Samantha Well, he said you and him...

Haley   What?!

Samantha He said you came on to him in a bar in town.

Haley   And you believe him?

Samantha I wasn't sure what to believe, it seemed so
incredible.

Haley   You should believe *me*.

Samantha I do, it's just / that

Haley   Just what?!

Samantha Well, I know what you're like after a few drinks
/ and

Haley   Flirting is one thing, but hitting on that idiot is
quite another.

Samantha So you *did* flirt with him?

Haley   That's not what I said.

Samantha So nothing happened? (*Pause*) Haley?

Haley   Nothing happened.

Samantha Because it didn't happen or because *you* / didn't
hit on *him*?

Haley   Because *I* didn't!

Haley sits down on the sofa.

Haley   It was my choice; he came on to me.

Samantha And you did nothing to encourage him?

Haley   Not really.

Samantha Haley?!

Haley I wanted to see how far he would go? I mean, I knew the two of you were over and fighting for custody, so I thought I'd see if I could provoke him.

Samantha Why would you do that?

Haley I was trying to help.

Samantha Well, you haven't.

Haley gets up.

Haley Look, you're my best friend and I'll always have your back. But marriages are never just one-sided. My mother could be a real bitch to my dad / you know.

Samantha He hit your mother.

Haley Only once.

Samantha That you know of.

Haley Life's not perfect. If it was, this wouldn't have happened to you.

Samantha No, but that doesn't mean we shouldn't try to make it the best it can be, even if it means walking away.

Haley Well, I just don't know if I'm the right person, then.

Haley leaves.

Samantha Haley.

SCENE 16

A weary Samantha is in the kitchen. Joe bursts in.

Joe   What's for tea?

Samantha Hi, Joe.

Joe   I got a message from Dad; he's asked if you can drop me off at his straight after football practice.

Samantha Sure, what do you want for tea?

Joe   I don't mind. Will it be long?

Samantha What about a takeaway?

Joe   Really?!

Samantha Just this once.

Joe   Can we get pizza?

Samantha Okay, but just a medium-size one each.

Samantha hands him the landline and takeaway flyer. Joe examines the pamphlet.

Joe   What about a Vegi Supreme? Can we have coleslaw...and potato wedges?

Samantha faints.

Joe   Mum? (*Turning to see she's not standing*) Mum!

SCENE 17

Samantha is sitting on the sofa clutching a glass of water. Joe sits nearby, staring at Samantha. Haley makes Joe a sandwich in the kitchen.

Haley	What did you think of the paramedics, Joe?
Joe	Good.
Haley	Do you still want your crusts off?
Joe	*No.*
Haley	You're still playing football, right? Centre midfield.
Joe	Centre-half.

Samantha realises that Joe is staring at her.

Samantha Joe, what are you doing, love?

Haley hands Joe his sandwich, which he eats.

Samantha	(*To Joe*) I'm sorry about the pizza. We'll have one on Saturday.
Joe	I'll still be at Dad's. Remember? You agreed I'd stay an extra night. I told you yesterday.
Samantha	Did you?
Joe	Yes!
Haley	Joe! Your mother's just fainted. I know you did well and everything calling the ambulance and me, but let her rest for a bit. (*To Samantha*) Are you sure you don't want anything?

Samantha I'm fine.

Haley Joe, you're going to have to take a bit of the weight off your mum's shoulders. She can't do everything herself / any more.

Joe She's said.

Samantha Haley, if you need to get home, that's okay.

Haley Well, if that's what you want?

Samantha Thanks, really.

Haley starts to tidy up.

Samantha Leave it. Joe will do it, won't you?

Joe What? Oh, yeah.

Haley prepares to leave.

Haley Will I see you at yoga on Sunday?

Samantha I'll do my best. I've got to see if I can get into work tomorrow first.

Haley I thought you weren't working Fridays any more.

Samantha That's right...but they're short-staffed, so I said I'd go in.

Haley Well, ring me if you need anything. You too, Joe.

Haley leaves.

Samantha How's the sandwich?

Joe Not bad.

SCENE 18

Joe is on his phone.

Joe   Hi Jens, how are you?...I'm sorry, I must have
           dialled the wrong...Oh, it is...Can I speak to
           Jens, please...I'm Joe...Yes, Joseph, like in the
           Bible...Who are...Jens' mother...Did he, that was
           nice of him...Can I speak to him?...Oh...oh,
           I thought...I thought if I phoned...it's only
           been a week, I didn't realise he was so ill...
           All his life...I'm sorry...No, I don't have any
           children, I'm fifteen...You're eighty-two...
           Wow!...No, I've never been to Denmark...Next
           week?...I'd like to come but I don't think I'd be
           allowed...I'll miss him too...Yes, he was a very
           good gamer...The best.

Joe ends the call.

SCENE 19

Joe enters in a rush, looking for something. Barry follows.

Joe   They're around here somewhere.

Barry enters the kitchen area. Joe stops.

Joe   Mum doesn't really want you to come inside
when she's not here.

Barry   Keep looking.

*Joe continues to look. Barry investigates, opening kitchen
drawers. He pulls out a letter. Joe finds the headset and observes
Barry reading the document.*

Joe   Don't.

Barry   *Dear Ms. Mallet.* She used to hate her maiden
name. *Further to your request for advice in
regards /*

Joe   You shouldn't even be in here.

Barry   *...to the care of your son, Josep Fielding, in the event
of your death or incapacitation. Unless the court felt
your son was in jeopardy, it's likely the court would
side towards his father, rather than the alternatives
you've /* suggested.

*Joe snatches the letter. Barry grabs him, pinning him against a
wall, and takes the letter and finishes reading it. He lets go of
Joe, then returns the letter to the drawer.*

Barry   Let's go.

Barry leaves, followed by a shaken Joe.

SCENE 20

Joe and Samantha are at home. Samantha rests on the sofa as Joe makes his own dinner. His phone rings, it's a video call.

Joe   (*Flustered*) Zoe?! Hold on.

In a panic, he pulls out some earphones and plugs them into the phone.

Joe   Hello...(*Touches cap*) Thanks...You went? No, I wouldn't have been allowed...How was it?...I see...I'll miss him too...Oh, I'm making dinner... Carbonara...Uh, she's resting...I'm quite good at cooking, actually...For you?...Sure...Next month?!

Samantha wakes.

Joe   I'll have to ask but...that would be great, I can show you around, there's the skate park and... sure, sure, no hurry... (*Realising Samantha has woken*) Look, I'd better go...Bye.

Samantha sits up.

Samantha Who was that, love?
Joe   No one special.

SCENE 21

Joe lies on the sofa, the cap low over his face. Samantha enters using the cane. Joe's sports bag sits on the breakfast bar.

Samantha I've told you before about putting this up here.
Joe I'll move it later.
Samantha What do you want for your tea?
Joe Don't mind. Do you need a hand?
Samantha I'm okay, but thanks for asking. What about shepherd's pie?

Samantha opens Joe's bag.

Joe Sure.
Samantha How's your dad?

Samantha examines the clean and folded clothes.

Joe Fine.
Samantha This makes a change.
Joe Tina did them. She's moved in.
Samantha That's quick.
Joe She's a gamer too. Boring turn-based stuff, though.
Samantha Isn't she a bit old for playing games?
Joe Jens wasn't.
Samantha No, you're right, love, I'm sorry.

Joe   Some people make a living out of it, you know?

Samantha But *you're* not going to do that, are you?

Joe   (*Quietly*) Maybe.

Samantha *Are* you?

Joe   No.

Samantha So, what do you want for your tea?

Joe   I said I *don't* mind.

Samantha moves towards him.

Samantha You did. Is everything okay?

Joe   Yes.

Samantha Will you take your cap off, please?

Joe   But...

Samantha Off!

Joe takes his cap off but turns away. Samantha sits next to him.

Samantha Face me.

Joe turns to face her.

Samantha (*Looking at his forehead*) What's that?!

Joe   Nothing.

Samantha It's nothing, is it? Joe, what happened?

Joe   I fell.

Samantha You fell. Doing what?

Joe   Playing football.

Samantha On a grass pitch?!

Joe No, the concrete. Outside the school.

Samantha I thought the Head had banned that?

Joe shrugs.

Samantha Are you telling me the truth?

Joe Don't you believe me?

Samantha What's going on? Did someone at school hit you?

No response from Joe. Samantha gets up.

Samantha I knew it. I'm phoning them right now.

She looks for the number on her phone and begins to dial.

Joe Stop. Stop!

Samantha Joe, I'm not having you getting into fights again. I thought all that had stopped. My bloody parents are going to have a field day after saying they'd pay for you to go to / a private school.

Joe It was Dad.

Samantha What? (*To the person on the phone*) Never mind.

Samantha ends the call.

Samantha Your father did that?

Joe He didn't mean to.

Samantha He's said that before. I'm calling the police.
Joe   Please don't.

Joe cries. Samantha goes to comfort him.

Samantha But Joe, if we don't...

Joe embraces her.

Samantha Okay, there, it's alright, we'll talk about that
              later. Let me get the first aid kit.

Samantha begins to move, but Joe holds her tight.

Samantha Okay, love. Everything's going to be okay.

SCENE 22

Samantha and Haley are sitting on the sofa.

Haley   Your lawyer thinks you should go to the police?
Samantha Well, otherwise it's just me repeating what Joe's
              told me.
Haley   And will you?
Samantha What else can I do? I thought things were going
              well between them and I could rely on Barry to
              take up most of the slack. But now he's shown
              he's still the same as he ever was, we'll have to.

Joe enters, unheard by them.

Haley   How do you think Joe'll feel about telling on his dad?

Joe   What's going on?

Samantha   Hi, Joe.

Haley   It's / nothing.

Samantha   No, it's okay. He can know. Joe, I spoke to the lawyer today. If we want to have it on record that your dad hit you, we'll need to go to the police station. How do you feel about that?

Joe   Isn't telling you enough?

Samantha   No, it's not.

Haley   Do you think the court will even do anything?

Samantha   Well, they might not, but if it happens again or Joe doesn't want to see his dad in the future / it's better to have a record of it.

Joe   But I do.

Samantha   But if you change your mind, we need something on record.

Joe   Would he find out?

Samantha   I'd imagine the police would want to speak to him.

Haley   I got interviewed once.

Samantha   You never told me / that.

Joe   What happened?

Haley   I was working behind the bar at the Student Union. Someone was skimming from the till. We

	all got called in and the police interviewed us all one by one. It took forever.
Samantha	Was it a lot of money?
Haley	Three and a half thousand pounds.
Joe	Wow!
Haley	There was just me and these two hunky policemen in this tiny room.
Joe	Were you scared?
Haley	I enjoyed it.
Samantha	I bet you did. What did you tell them?
Haley	I said I didn't know anything, of course.
Joe	Did they catch the thief?
Haley	Never.
Samantha	*And*?
Haley	What? Sure, I had a few dates with one of them. Errol. He was tall, with cobalt eyes, just like yours, Joe. (*To Samantha*) Don't you remember, I thought he was *the one*?
Samantha	And that was the end of it?
Haley	Sort of.
Joe	(*To Haley*) Was it you, Haley? Did you take the money?
Haley	No, Joe, how could you think that? But I knew who did.
Samantha	And you said nothing?
Joe	*Never rat on your friends and always keep your mouth shut.*
Samantha	Where did you hear that?

Joe   Jens. He said it was from a movie called
             Goodfellas. He said I should see it. Can I, Mum?

Samantha No. Haley, I can't believe you would / do that.

Joe   I think it's cool.

Samantha It's certainly not that.

Samantha gets up with the use of the cane.

Samantha Right, that's it, we're making a statement.

Joe   Mum!

Samantha I'm sorry, Joe, but you'll have / to.

Joe   Haley?

Haley   Come on, Sam, if he doesn't want to.

Samantha (*To Haley*) You've been enough help today,
             thank you. I'll ring the station in the morning,
             see if we can go in after you've finished school.

Joe   But...

Samantha Why don't you start on your homework? I'll call
             you when dinner's ready.

Joe leaves.

Samantha (*To Haley*) Thanks.

SCENE 23

Haley's in the kitchen cooking and drinking wine as Joe enters.

Haley	Hey, Joe.
Joe	Hi, Haley.
Haley	Your mum told you I'd be here, didn't she?
Joe	Yeah.
Haley	What do you want for your tea?
Joe	Don't mind.

Joe goes to the sofa.

Haley	I do a mean spinach and chickpea soup. (*No response*) Luckily enough, I expected that response and that is why we're having veggie spag bol.
Joe	Sounds alright.
Haley	How was school?
Joe	Okay.
Haley	Yep, that's how I remember it. Right, should just be a few more minutes.

Haley sits on the sofa next to Joe.

Haley	So, how are things with the ladies?
Joe	What?
Haley	Have you got a girlfriend?

Joe   Not really.

Haley   So, there is someone?

Joe   Zoe. She's in the co-op team I used to be in. We've been messaging.

Haley   (*Indicates lips*) And have you?

Joe   We've not met yet.

Haley   Slow burner, eh? Well, it might help if she could see your face when you meet.

Haley takes off Joe's cap and moves his hair from his face.

Haley   You are going to meet, aren't you?

Joe   This weekend.

Haley   There, that's better, isn't it, even *with* the bruise. With these beautiful eyes, how can anyone fail to want to kiss you?

They stay motionless. Something tips over on the cooker.

Joe   Something's wrong in the kitchen.

Haley   Right...Oh right!

Haley rushes to the stove.

Joe   Haley, do you think Mum's going to be okay?

Haley   Of course she will. They can do amazing things nowadays. I heard they've got this new thing where they take out your cells, supercharge

	them, then stick them back in. She'll be fine, you'll see.
Joe	I'm worried.
Haley	So am I, Joe, but it's okay to be worried. We're worried because we both love her. Why don't you come over here and help me?

Joe goes to Haley.

Haley	Now, your mum's probably never told you this trick, but the best way to tell if spaghetti is done is to see if it sticks to something.

Haley takes a strand of spaghetti and hurls it against the wall.

Haley	You try.

Joe throws a strand.

Joe	Can I have another go?

Haley and Joe, laughing raucously, throw spaghetti against the wall and then each other, unaware that Samantha has returned, standing there, looking on disapprovingly.

SCENE 24

Joe's reading on the sofa without his cap. The kitchen's a mess.
Samantha enters using her cane.

Samantha Hello?

Joe jumps up excitedly.

Joe Hi.

Samantha Been busy, I see?

Joe begins to tidy up.

Joe I'll clear it up.

Samantha Someone was hungry.

Joe We got carried away.

Samantha What's she like, then?

Joe Alright.

Samantha Just alright?

Joe You'd like her.

Samantha It seemed like you didn't want me to meet her.

Joe She didn't have much time, like I said.

Samantha So, what did you get up to?

Joe Not much. We talked and I found out she's
thinking of doing similar A levels to me.
Although they're called something different
in Belgium. They're called...anyway, I can't

145

remember. Then we went online, chatted for a bit, then I made dinner. She helped. She's really good at it. Then we just sat around.

Samantha Sat around, eh?

Joe Uh-huh.

Samantha As long as you had a good time.

Joe She left something for you. Because I told her how you were really into art and everything.

Joe hands Samantha a black ink drawing.

Samantha Well, I'm not sure where we'll put it.

Joe If you don't have room for it...I can look after it for you in my room.

Samantha That's kind of you.

Joe snatches the picture back.

Samantha Just a loan, mind.

Joe Sure.

Samantha I think you've got some clearing up to do.

Joe starts cleaning up while Samantha moves to the sofa.

Joe Mum.

Samantha Yes, Joe.

Joe Is it easy to get to Brussels?

SCENE 25

Samantha's waiting in the kitchen as Joe arrives back from
football practice. She watches him settle down.

Samantha I was called into your school today. Do you
know why?

Joe No.

Samantha Mrs Roper said there'd been a fight. A boy was
beaten quite badly and had to go to hospital.
The teacher said he had it coming to him,
but that's beside the point. They still have to
investigate. The boy and his friends, well, they
aren't saying who did it, but you'd been seen
arguing with them earlier. Had you?

Joe I don't remember.

Samantha She also said you were told to give me a note to call
the school. Why didn't you give me the note, Joe?

Joe I didn't want you to know.

Samantha Joe!

Joe I'm sorry.

Samantha What happened?

Joe Nothing.

Samantha Don't lie to me, what was it about?

Joe Nothing!

Joe's upset and goes to the sofa. Samantha sits next to him and
comforts him.

Samantha Whatever it is, it can't be that bad. The boy's going to be okay, he'll be back at school next week.

Joe I wish he was dead.

Samantha Don't say that. What is it, love?

Joe I don't want to tell you.

Samantha Your father didn't really hit you, did he?

Joe shakes his head.

Samantha Oh, Joe.

Joe I'm sorry.

Samantha Tell me what really happened.

Joe It was about you.

Samantha Me?

Joe agrees.

Samantha What was it about?

Joe They'd seen you pick me up from school. Using the cane. They said...they said...

Samantha What did they say?

Joe That you were a *spaz* and going to die.

Samantha Right, well, that's...I suppose the saying about 'sticks and stones' didn't come into your head at this point.

Joe I didn't mean to hurt him. He hit me too.

Samantha I know, love. Well, it's happened now, so we're just going to have to deal with it.

Samantha gets up, looks at the letter, then makes a call.

Joe   What are you doing?

Samantha I'm going to speak to Mrs. Roper and tell her you were involved. Then I'm going to call my lawyer and then the police station.

Joe   Can't it wait?

Samantha I suppose it could.

SCENE 26

Samantha puts some bread in the toaster, then goes to the sofa and logs in.

Samantha Hi, Zoe...No, Joe's not here at the moment, he's with his dad...Don't worry about it, I know you had a train to catch...Is he? Well, maybe I'll ask him to cook for /

The lights go out and the gaming system turns off.

Samantha ...me.

Samantha stumbles to the fuse box. She resets the system and the lights come back on. Barry's standing there.

Samantha Jesus!

Barry   Hello, Sam.

Samantha   What do you want?

Barry   I could ask you the same thing.

Samantha   What are you talking about?

Barry   I had a visit from the police *and* a letter from your lawyer.

Samantha   About that...

Barry   He's a liar.

Samantha   I know. I only just found out. I was going to call / later.

Barry   Later! The letter said you'd be asking for my time with Joe to be reduced. Did you ask him to lie?

Samantha   No! How can you say that?

Barry   You'd do anything to get what you want?

Samantha   And *you* wouldn't?

Barry   I wouldn't lie. What was he thinking?

Samantha   He was worried about getting suspended from school again. That bruise was from a fight.

Barry   I thought that'd all stopped.

Samantha   Some boys on the football team were teasing him. I wouldn't be surprised if he gave up playing after this. I think he only went because you used to play. I still can't believe he'd lie, though.

Barry   Can't you?

Samantha   He hasn't lied to me before, at least not about anything important.

Barry   And you believe that?

Samantha   Of course?

Barry   Remember those fish you had? The little sparkly
               ones that swam about in a group?

Samantha   Guppies, but there were others / too.

Barry   They all died, didn't they?

Samantha   There was something wrong with the water or
               the filter, I can't recall. So what?

Barry   Joe put bleach in the tank.

Samantha   You're lying.

Barry   Why would I?

Samantha   To get back at Joe for accusing you. Why didn't
               you say anything at the time?

Barry   Because I knew how upset you'd be if you
               thought Joe wasn't perfect.

Samantha   I used to think you were, but it didn't take long
               to figure out the truth.

Barry   No one's perfect, Sam, especially not you.

Samantha   What do you mean?

Barry   Haley's policeman. Errol, wasn't it?

Samantha   What are you talking about?

Barry   Errol and I played Sunday football together for
               a bit, before he moved boroughs. Funny how
               a few choice words can turn someone against
               someone else. He didn't tell me what you said
               about Haley, but it was enough to dump her. I
               told him it wasn't true, but by then it was too
               late. Why would you do that?

Samantha   I was looking out for her.

Barry   Is that what you call it? And are you looking out for Joe, spreading his lies?

Samantha I said I was going to sort it out.

Barry   I should have seen it a long time ago. All through our marriage, you made *me* out to be the villain.

Samantha You did that yourself.

Barry grips her around the throat.

Samantha Go on, do it!

Barry lets go.

Barry   You'd like that, wouldn't you? It would suit you down to the ground. To have Joe all to yourself. Making everything revolve around you, everyone at your beck and call. I wouldn't be surprised if you're not even ill.

Samantha Of course I am.

Barry   I mean, you work in an outpatient clinic. You could easily make the paperwork look real. Create fake test results. You always hated it when I had to work away. You guilt-tripped me into quitting that job.

Samantha Don't be ridiculous, you never liked working there.

Barry   And Haley, I never understood why you stayed friends with her. You're nothing alike and you've always known she can't be trusted with anything requiring a grown-up. But if you need her, she comes running.

Samantha Leave her out of this.

Barry What about Joe? You always said you didn't think life would be worth living if Joe ever left home.

Samantha You're talking rubbish. You just can't bear the thought that you might not get to see him.

Barry I didn't hit him and never would. You know, when he killed your fish, I couldn't understand how anyone could do that. But now I can see it. It's you, in him. God help Joe if he becomes even more like you.

Samantha Better me than a bully who thinks they can persuade people with their fists.

Barry At least my way's out in the open.

Samantha Get out.

Barry leaves.

SCENE 27

Samantha and Joe are getting ready to leave the house.

Samantha Now, you're sure you've got everything?

Joe Yes.

Samantha spots Joe's headset.

Samantha What about your headset?

Joe Zoe said we should have a weekend without it.

Samantha And you agreed?

Joe nods.

Samantha Well. Now, your dad said he'd talk to you about, you know, sex and stuff.

Joe He didn't have time.

Samantha He promised. We've got time, sit / down.

Joe Mum, we did sex ed at school last term.

Samantha That's right, you did. But you'll be careful, won't you?

Joe Yes!

Samantha You're too young anyway, it'd be illegal.

Joe Can we go now?!

Joe picks up his luggage. Samantha takes her handbag.

Samantha You've never been away on your own before.

Joe It's *only* Brussels.

Samantha You're growing up so fast. Promise me you'll never leave me.

Joe *Mum*, let's go.

Samantha Okay, okay.

Samantha goes first.

Joe   Mum, you forgot your cane.

Joe takes it, shutting the door.

SCENE 28

Samantha lies on the sofa, a blanket over her legs. The television is on.

Joe returns, lifting his luggage onto the breakfast bar. The cane, resting against it, falls to the floor. Samantha murmurs.

Joe   Mum?

Joe turns off the television, then pulls the blanket up to cover her chest. He picks up the cane, turning to look at his mother.

End.

LOUD MOUTH

Loud Mouth **was written between 2016 and 2020.**

CHARACTERS ///
DAVID MAYHEW: WHITE, MALE, 30S
AMARI: BLACK, FEMALE, 30S
JENNY: BLACK, FEMALE, 16
POLICE COMMUNITY SUPPORT OFFICER: 20S

SETTING ///
A RADIO STATION

AUTHOR'S NOTES ///
/ INDICATES OVERLAP

ACT 1

SCENE 1

The stage is black. It's raining hard, thunder cracks and water drips into a metal waste bin like a metronome. Someone enters in a wheelchair and hits the light switch. It flickers briefly but fails to stay on.

He crosses the stage and switches on a lamp, revealing a desk, microphone and computer. Behind are three windows with blackout blinds. David Mayhew hangs a gold necklace over the lamp and cleans his hands.

David moves behind the desk, puts on headphones and clicks the mouse. An ON AIR light goes on.

David   You're hooked into Liberty Radio on Two Zero Two, sight and sound delivered straight into your brain via HALO, the new standard for sound and vision. This is your shock jock with the big cock bringing you your random check-in with reality. It's the end of the world as we know it, but that's where you get the best view. So buckle up, chow down and embrace the darkest corners of your mind. Like a laser beam from a killer queen, I'll be slicing and dicing through your head, lighting you up and turning your insides out. Slip on your headphones or hide under the bedclothes, but whatever you do, know that I'm coming for you. Prisoner or passenger, it's your choice. In this post-Change world, what does this mean for you? We'll be taking calls, so you can tell me. But now for the main event. Never knowingly beaten, consistently irregular, the one and only, the master of mayhem, a floating point of order, me, David. Let's clear our minds and get this party started.

David triggers a track. He takes off the headphones and throws up into the bin. He reads a local newspaper from the top of a pile. The song ends.

David   Looks like we're being blessed. Listen to this: (*reading from paper*) "At the end of the month, the Community Centre will become the country's twenty-second Rehabilitation Unit for those affected by The Change. The state-funded activity provides training and support to the millions of young people affected." Typical. On our doorstep, ruining the neighbourhood. No consultation. State intervention at its finest. A knife-like incision into our community's heart. And we're just meant to sit here and take it. We need to stick up for ourselves, show them that we don't want them here. We need help, not them. Our economic future, bollocks. We don't need them. I don't need them. They shouldn't be here.

David checks the screen.

David   Thanks, PiratePete. Milly says, "It's about time someone said what we were all thinking." And teenterror273 writes to say, "I'm a tosser and should be taken off the air." Well, thanks, but I ain't going nowhere. I certainly ain't running scared. How's everyone doing out there, are we up for some calls? Light them up, baby!...Hello, caller. What's your name and what's your point?... John, you're all called John, aren't you?...Well, John, what can we do? I'll tell you what we can do. We tell our politicians we don't want them. We don't need them. We can look after ourselves. We're a nation of inventors, aren't we? There's new technology: augmentation, stem cell resets, robotics. These youngsters were still in short pants during the worst of it: losing friends, parents, grandparents. We pulled together and now bear the scars. Still here. Alive. But that doesn't mean I want some fresh-faced teenager sticking their nose into my business. I can still wipe my own ass, thank you. Next caller...Yes, Gulshan, we can't be having them lording it over us, telling us what's best for us. "Don't drive. Retire. You've put that in the wrong bin." Next caller...Politicians - bunch of bastards, I agree, Oskar. Couldn't organise a blow job in a brothel. You're right, it's not too late to stop them. Have a party...no, a movement. This is about how we live our lives. We need to push back. Rattle some pots, ruffle some feathers. Let them know we were here first and we're not going quietly into the night.

David cues a track. He cuts out the article and sticks it to a wall. The track ends.

David   Next caller...Next caller, you're on air.

Jenny   (*Quietly*) Hello.

David   You'll need to speak up. What's your name and what's your point?

Jenny   My point?

David   What's getting you riled?

Jenny   Nothing.

David   Something must be bothering you...Your name's not showing up, glitch in the matrix or something. What is it?

Jenny   Jenny. Yes, it's Jenny.

David   You don't sound too sure.

Jenny   No, I know now. It's Jenny.

David   What's on your mind?

Jenny   I don't know what to do.

David   Done something bad, have we?

Jenny   I'm not like that.

David   How old are you?

Jenny   Fourteen.

David   Sounds about right. Were you affected by it?

Jenny   I don't know.

David   Where are you calling from?

Jenny   I'm not sure.

David   How can you not know where you are? Look, if you don't have anything useful to say, I'm cutting you off.

Jenny   Don't! There's someone else here.

David   Well, maybe they can help you find a way out. Goodbye.

David ends the call.

David   Sorry about that, folks, I think she meant to call Radio Uno. Some music to shake off the holier-than-thou stench that's filled the air.

Music plays. David takes out his phone and rings someone.

David   Gerry...Yes, I know I'm on, so it will need to be quick...This topic has hit a nerve, I know...Look, I can trust you, can't I?... Yeah, I know I shouldn't have to ask but...Okay, okay...If you needed to get rid of a car...That's right...Where would you dump it?...Behind the biorefinery...I know it...Ta...No, everything's all right...Will be...I'll ring you once it's done, pick me up somewhere nearby...Thanks... Look, gotta go.

David finishes the call and cues music. He cuts out headlines from the papers and pastes them to the walls. He returns to the desk.

David   That's the last one from me tonight. Places to be and all that. So, till next time, time bandits. Sayonara.

The ON AIR light goes out. David turns off the desk lamp and leaves.

Jenny   Hello, is anyone there?

SCENE 2

David arrives with a bag of items taken from a car, plus a newspaper with a girl's face on the front. He switches on the main light.

David   Morning, campers, how are we this fine day? I passed through one of our villages last night. You know, one of those that seems not to have changed for centuries. Church on one side, all that. I thought of all those baptisms, marriages and burials that must have happened. On the other side, an empty field. Or at least it should've been. Instead: blue plastic bottles, bags stuck in hedges and sandwich packets with their lids flapping like crocodiles. All this from our gifted generation.

David plays a track.

David   Let's take a call. System's playing up again, but I think I have you. Right, caller, what's your name and what's your point?

Jenny   It's Jenny.

David   Again. But still, it ain't against the rules, I guess. Do you know where you are today?

Jenny   I'm with you.

David   Funny. What do you think about the litter problem?

Jenny   I don't like it.

David   No one likes it, but what should we do about it?

Jenny   Educate people that it's not right.

David   Coming from the generation that learns at Mach Three, that's a bit rich. Action is what we need. Punish the transgressors.

Jenny   I think we're all responsible.

David   We'll have to agree to disagree. Maybe you'd like to stick up for your kind?

Jenny   My kind?

David   Let's keep it simple for you. Have you been moved out of your school?

Jenny   Yes, to a Rehabilitation Unit. To study medicine.

David   Why medicine?

Jenny   I like to look after people.

David   What if we don't want looking after?

Jenny   Why wouldn't you want that?

David   Because I'm not ready to be put back in nappies. To have to pass a test to drive every year. I'll need your permission just to take a piss next. You're too young to remember what it was like. Not knowing what might happen. What we thought would happen, didn't. What did was worse.

Jenny   We studied it.

David   That's not the same as feeling it.

Jenny   I don't understand.

David   I'm not sure I can help you then, and right now, you're sucking all the life out of my show.

Jenny   I didn't realise that's what this was. Is that why it's black with the white and red lights?

David ends the call.

David   I'm sorry, caller, we've lost you.

He cues a track. He throws some items into the bin.
The track ends.

David   Actions speak louder than words, they say. But what if you only have words? What do you do then? You call on others for help. Those of passion, common spirit. Those that will protest, make placards, bang pots and more. Protest on behalf of those that can't. Brothers and sisters in arms. Boots on the ground. An army of the disenfranchised, forgotten by the state too eager to rebuild an economy with fresh faces, throwing the rest of us on the scrapheap. Who's with me?

David checks the monitor.

David   It appears I'm not alone. Matthew from Derby, "Just tell me where." Juliette from Newquay, "I'm with you all the way." An adults' army, fighting injustice. Well, let me tell you, it's not too late to make a stand. And I know just where to start.

David plays a track, pushes away from the desk and dances.

SCENE 3

David sits in front of the windows. A crowd moves past outside, chanting anti-youth slogans.

SCENE 4

Music plays as David packs to leave. Amari Wells enters.

Amari Hello. Are you David?

David How did you get in?

Amari The door was open. It's not what I expected.

David What were you expecting?

Amari Something bigger.

David This is all you need to reach the world now. HALO needs gigaspeed bandwidth of course, but when the Community Centre got upgraded, I took advantage.

Amari Rehabilitation Unit.

David Sorry?

Amari It's now a Rehabilitation Unit for those affected. It's still open to those living nearby, if you want to drop in.

David Would I be welcome?

Amari Of course.

David But they're there. (*Pause*) You know.

Amari Freaks. Mutants. Monsters. Deviants. / Aberrations.

David Okay, okay. They're not the terms I'd use.

Amari Just your supporters. We had to smuggle them out of the back to be collected by their parents.

David I'm surprised they still need them.

Amari They're children.

David If they don't want to grow up so fast / then...

Amari They didn't choose what happened to them.

David   Nor did I.

Amari   I'm sorry, I didn't know, but is it really necessary?

David   We've got the right to make our feelings known.

Amari   Some of them might not come back and most can't go back to their old schools. What are they supposed to do? They need help.

David   And we don't?

Amari   There's support, isn't there?

David   An oh-eight-hundred number. If you're not contributing to the state, you're a drain on it. "If you could just hold this anchor as you leap into the water, it would be much obliged."

Amari   Well, I'm not saying I agree with it all, but some of us are doing the best we can.

David   They're lucky to have you.

Amari   So how does all this work?

David   I was about to leave.

Amari   Do you live nearby?

David   Walking distance. You can laugh, it is allowed.

Amari examines the desk.

Amari   It looks complex.

David   Not really. Once you've selected your playlist and meta tags, the HALO system pretty much runs the show, adapting to each listener's preferences.

Amari   I tried it at a friend's. It always seems to pick the right images.

David   Millions of data points. Every click, word written or post you've ever made, transformed into floating images, matching the music. There's transmitters here too, but they're not working. Anyway, I'm sure you're not here to learn about this. Why are you here?

Amari   You were mentioned at the rally.

David   Good to know I have at least one fan out there.

Amari   Quite a few actually. Why weren't you there?

David   More of a backseat driver.

Amari   I listened to your show.

David   I don't have any stickers, I'm afraid.

Amari   How can you blame them for what happened to you?

David   I know they're not the cause. But they're not the solution either.

Amari   And you think aggression's the answer?

David   All they have to do is leave.

Amari   They've been affected as much as you.

David   You're kidding, aren't you? They won the lottery compared to me.

Amari   They don't see it that way.

David   Is there anything else?

Amari   Will they be back tomorrow?

David   Do you think it matters what I say?

Amari   You might want to save them a trip. The RU's shut tomorrow.

David   Day off, is it?

Amari   As a mark of respect for one of their cohort: Jenny.
She was killed by a hit-and-run driver last week.
Her funeral's tomorrow.

SCENE 5

*A policeman enters the studio and approaches the desk. David
emerges from the toilet.*

PCSO   It was open, I hope that's okay?

David   (*Quietly*) Might as well have a swing door.

PCSO   Sorry?

David   How can I help?

PCSO   Is this where you broadcast from?

David   Yes.

PCSO   Looks complicated.

David   Very. Just passing, were you?

PCSO   You're on my route, sir.

David   Must be nice to wander about, popping into places
whenever you feel like it, checking everything's
okay.

PCSO   It's set to be different every day.

David   I feel privileged to be on it, then. If it's about the
rally, I wasn't there.

PCSO   It's about your car.

David   My car?

PCSO   A red Ford Hydro. It was found near the industrial
estate. Pretty beat up, I'm afraid. Kids used it for

target practice. You'll want it back I expect, because of the modifications.

David Where do I sign?

PCSO You'll get a text when it's ready for collection.

David How modern, thanks.

PCSO If you need to contact me, here's my number.

The PCSO hands David a card.

PCSO Why didn't you report it missing?

David I only just realised it was gone.

PCSO That model's got an impact tracker built in. You should've got an alert when it hit the bank?

David Technology, eh? Is that all?

PCSO One more thing. In regards the Rehabilitation Unit next door, it reopens tomorrow. Can I take it the youngsters will be safe?

David If it was up to me, they'd have nothing to worry about.

SCENE 6

David is on a phone call as Amari enters.

David Look, Gerry, I've got to go. I must do something about that door.

Amari You never know who might come in.

David What do you want?

Amari I wanted to thank you.

David Really?

Amari For what you said on the radio?

David That our re-education policy is a waste of taxpayers' money? That those of us affected are angry at this fawning over the special ones? That this has only led to division?

Amari For asking them not to protest yesterday. There's some graffiti, but it's being removed. I think you said if someone was to do it, it would be "a waste of ink".

David It would, it is. If we want to have a real discussion about the impacts of human redundancy on a national scale, we need to do more than daub a slogan on a wall.

Amari Why do you feel this way?

David What way?

Amari Your dislike of young people.

David You misunderstand me, I don't like most older people either. Is there something else?

Amari Aren't you going to ask about the funeral?

David Why should I? Now, if you don't mind.

Amari leaves.

David turns off the table lamp.

The light turns back on. He switches it back off and heads to the door, turning off the main light.

Jenny   Hello.

David   What do you want?

Jenny   To talk.

David   What if I don't want to?

Jenny   Why don't you want to talk to me?

David   Because you're dead!

The lamp turns on.

David   Parlour tricks don't impress me.

Jenny   Why didn't you see me?

David   You came out of nowhere.

Jenny   You were driving too fast.

David   You weren't paying attention.

Jenny   You should have seen me. / I'd be alive if you had.
You weren't paying attention. You should have seen
me. Seen me. Me. Me. ME.

David   I tried to stop. I did. But it was wet and dark. I was tired.
I tried to stop. Please stop. Please. Stop. Stop. STOP.

The lamp turns off.

SCENE 7

David is at the desk, on air.

David   Welcome to those with nowhere to go. To those
pushed out of their jobs, relegated to the scrap-heap

of life. Come all who dare to fight the good fight.
The battle approaches. Last week was but a skirmish.
A warm-up. Do not be afraid to lose your liberty.
If we do nothing, it will be taken from us. Do what
I can't and make me proud. Those that sacrifice
themselves today will be welcomed as the saviours
of tomorrow. Drive them out, for they seek not
only to replace us but to relegate us, so we're but a
shadow of ourselves. Act now to stop the infestation.
Good luck and God speed.

*David plays a track. There is the sound of marching outside.
Crowds chant loudly. Police sirens wail. David faces the
windows. There's an explosion and yellow-orange light floods
around the blinds. Chants of "Mayhew/Mayhem" ring out.*

SCENE 8

*David sleeps on the floor. The desk lamp itself turns on.
He wakes.*

David   Is that you?

Jenny   Yes.

David   You woke me.

Jenny   I needed to speak to you.

David   What time is it?

Jenny   Three. Maybe four.

David   The suicide hour. What's it like where you are?

Jenny Scary. I don't like it.

David Why don't you leave, then?

Jenny I don't know how.

Jenny cries.

David Do I frighten you?

Jenny What you're doing does.

David It's none of your concern.

Jenny Burning everything to the ground won't bring you peace.

David It's the only way.

Jenny You know it's not.

David Leave me alone. Get out of my head!

The bulb on the desk burns very bright, then goes out.

ACT 2

SCENE 9

There's a knock. David opens the door and the PCSO enters.
David fixes a lock on the door.

PCSO   Good afternoon.

David   Not any more.

PCSO   I'd like to talk to you about the events of yesterday.

David   Why, did something happen?

PCSO   There was a demonstration yesterday that became violent. There's been significant damage to the building.

David   What's it got to do with me?

PCSO   Your HALO transmissions have been cited as a contributor to the motivations of many of those that attended.

David   *Mens rea* or *actus reus*?

PCSO   Sorry?

David   If I'm to be arrested for inciting violence, is it *mens rea* or *actus reus*? Or both, although I'm not sure that's possible. Anyway, if it's *actus reus*, you'd need to prove that I encouraged a specific action. If it's *mens rea*, that I knew it would be committed. Did I comment on the fact that I was unhappy with my neighbours? Sure. But in terms of specific actions, I don't think there's much to go on.

PCSO   Encouraging or assisting a crime is a serious offence.

David holds out his hands.

David   So arrest me. You won't though, will you, even if
you could? You know you're looking at things the
wrong way. I mean, who's most at fault: the state
that authorises the partitioning of individuals
based on a once in-a-lifetime event, or the half
who make their feelings known?

PCSO   With due respect, they did more than that. It wasn't
a simple case of some graffiti and a sit-in, sir. The
fire damage runs into the thousands. It's unclear
whether the building will be able to reopen.

David   Shame.

PCSO   I'd like to make sure it doesn't happen again.

David   And I have some say in that, do I?

PCSO   I'm led to believe you do.

David   And if I don't play ball?

PCSO   Criminal charges will be brought.

David   Thanks for clearing that up. Now if there's nothing
else, I've a lock to fit.

The PCSO leaves and Amari enters.

David   Come in, one and all.

Amari   What did they want?

David   To give me a friendly warning.

Amari And will you listen?

David If they listen to us, I might.

Amari They told you about the damage?

David Yes.

Amari Is that all you can say?

David Something was bound to give in the end.

Amari You're despicable.

David I dare say you're right.

Amari Isn't it in all our interests to find a way of living with what's happened? You're not the only one who's been affected.

David When I got the diagnosis, I ignored it. It was just pins and needles. They could be wrong, I thought. But when I fell on the floor getting out of bed and couldn't get up, there was no denying it. I stayed home. Work kept phoning, then friends and family before they started banging on the door. I ignored them. Stared at the wall, mostly. I wanted to figure this out on my own. I'd try to walk across the room but would just black out. You know when you sit up too fast and get dizzy? Imagine that, times a hundred. I'm used to it now. And this thing. Even the pain. I couldn't do my job any more, but the pay-off allowed me to set up this. I don't get much for each stream, but it's building. Plus being here, I don't have to deal with the looks. People think they're being polite: "What happened?" "My friend's friend's in a wheelchair." You brush it off, but what you really want to do is run away. But you're stuck, talking to some gibbering idiot, looking down on you like you're a child. So what if there are others? There's only me inside this body that feels like someone else's. So sure, I'm not the only one, but that doesn't make it any easier.

Amari   Jenny's cohort were at her funeral. Only one of her old school friends came: Marianne. She said the rest thought Jenny was a freak. One day like them, then not. I've been doing this most of my life and never seen anything like it. I was a social worker before and there's some things you don't forget: maggots on food, babies in their own filth for days, the abuse and neglect. You develop a hard shell. You have to, otherwise you'd never go back to work. But it gets thicker, fusing to your skin so it feels like it will never come off. But you should feel something. So now I do this. There are still tough days. Kids coming in straight from school because they don't want to go home. You have to push them out the door at the end of the night. God knows what to do. I explain there's help, but most don't take it. These new kids, they're old before their time. But there's something else – bright, sure, but...At the funeral, amid the crying and hugging, they stood there, shoulder to shoulder, just staring down into the grave. And when it was over, their faces were dry.

David   They're not normal.

Amari   Is anyone after this? Jenny's parents asked them if
they'd seen something of Jenny's that's missing.
Blamed the police for not looking hard enough. It
isn't valuable. A necklace, with her name on the back.

Amari examines the necklace.

Amari   Like this one: a dolphin over a rainbow.

David grabs it from the lamp.

David   Probably lots like it. You know what kids are like
with trends.
Amari   Odd for a man to have something like that, though.
Especially when he doesn't wear any jewellery.

David gives her the necklace.

David   Take it. / Go on, take it. I don't want it any more.
Amari   No, why? No, stop, what are you doing?!

David falls out of his chair.

David   No! I don't need any help. Leave me alone. I just
want everyone to leave me alone.

Amari leaves with the necklace.

SCENE 10

David comes out of the bathroom to find Jenny waiting.

David   What are you doing here? You don't exist unless
I want you to. I know that now. And I don't, so
leave. Leave! What do you want from me? Say
something. I didn't see you, I'm sorry. I've given
your necklace back. They'll work it out, won't
they? Come for me. She'll give it to them. "Here's
a necklace from that bigot in the wheelchair
stirring things up. It's got her name on the back,
must be hers."

David phones someone.

David   Hi, Gerry. I know, in a portacabin...No, no plan...I
don't want to be involved any more...I can't...I'll
still do the show, but just music, nothing else...
No, I'm sorry, I've had enough.

David ends the call.

David   Happy now? Got what you wanted. I'm out of it. If
they keep going, it's nothing to do with me. I'm
neutral. Switzerland. I'm not to blame for what
happens next. So you can go now. Exit the building.
I've given you what you want, haven't I?

The table lamp and ceiling light burn bright. The table lamp's bulb explodes.

Jenny's gone.

SCENE 11

David screws a new bulb into the table lamp. He opens the blinds to muted daylight. There's a knock on the door.

David   It's open.

Amari enters.

David   How's the coven?

Amari   They don't seem to mind the new classroom. Can't say I ever expected to be working in a portacabin. With the protests winding down, they're a lot calmer, as much as anyone can tell. We're going to try some role playing next week. Recreate some social situations.

David   Did you give Jenny's parents the necklace?

Amari   No.

David   Why not?

Amari   How could I? You didn't say how you got it.

David   Does it matter?

Amari   I can't give them her necklace without knowing how you got it.

David   Do you expect me to confess to something?

Amari   Do you want to?

David   I'm tired of fighting.

Amari   Then stop. Stop all this. Let someone else take over, if you're not up for it.

David   I'm not saying that. I've nothing left to say.

Amari   And you think that will work? You think not asking for help will make things better?

David   It'll have to.

Amari   Jenny's school friend, Marianne, came into the RU today. She's mildly affected but not enough to join. Stuck between two worlds, poor thing. She told me she was there the night Jenny was killed.

David   So?

Amari   Jenny was telling Marianne about her new friends in the RU. Marianne was jealous, but Jenny didn't understand. The more Marianne tried to explain, the more she got frustrated with Jenny's attitude. Told her she was a robot. Jenny ran off, straight into the road. Marianne blames herself.

David   I'm due on air.

Amari   I'll go then.

David   No. Stay.

David directs Amari to look over his shoulder. He goes on air.

David   Hey, what's cooking? It's the bug in your ear, the fly in your soup and the stone in your shoe. I'm rattling the tin as hard as I can for your attention, one last time. Before we crank up the music for the Mayhew massive, the disenfranchised, the forgotten and those caught in the crossfire, I've a final message. What we believe in hasn't changed. That to be discarded, to be side-tracked and passed over, isn't fair. They get that now. Backing off is not backing down. But sometimes we need to think about where the blame lies. The state bears the brunt, and those that've benefited haven't shown us much sympathy. But we need to remember, they're kids. Fucked up, super-powered ones, but nonetheless kids. Who make mistakes too. And we were them once and not one of us wants to go back to acne and bullying in the schoolyard, do we? We can't put our troubles on their puny shoulders, however much it makes us feel better. It won't make it go away. That silent scream that swallows you. We have to accept that The Change affected us all. And we all have to make the best of what we've been left with. I may be gone a while, but I have a feeling you'll be in safe hands. So until I'm back to pop your cherry, wipe the smile from your face or party with you like it's our last night on Earth, peace be with you.

David takes off his headphones. He picks up his phone.

Amari   I'll go now.

Amari leaves. David holds the PCSO's card and dials.

David   Hello. It's David. I've something to tell you.

Lights out.

CPSIA information can be obtained
at www.ICGtesting.com
Printed in the USA
BVHW030934161221
624197BV00006B/242